PRACTICE - ASSESS - DIAGNO

180 Days of PROBLEM SOLVING
for Sixth Grade

? Think

🔑 Plan

💡 Solve

🔍 Explain

-3 > -10

Author
Stacy Monsman, M.A.

SHELL EDUCATION

For information on how this resource meets national and other state standards, see pages 4–7. You may also review this information by visiting our website at www.teachercreatedmaterials.com/administrators/correlations/ and following the on-screen directions.

Publishing Credits

Corinne Burton, M.A.Ed., *Publisher*; Conni Medina, M.A.Ed., *Managing Editor*; Emily R. Smith, M.A.Ed., *Series Developer*; Diana Kenney, M.A.Ed., NBCT, *Content Director*; Paula Makridis, M.A.Ed., *Editor*; Lee Aucoin, *Sr. Multimedia Designer*; Kyleena Harper, *Assistant Editor*; Kevin Pham, *Graphic Designer*

Image Credits

All images from iStock and Shutterstock.

Standards

Shell Education

A division of Teacher Created Materials
5301 Oceanus Drive
Huntington Beach, CA 92649-1030

www.tcmpub.com/shell-education
ISBN 978-1-4258-1618-6
©2017 Shell Education Publishing, Inc.

TABLE OF CONTENTS

INTRODUCTION

The Need for Practice

To be successful in today's mathematics classrooms, students must deeply understand both concepts and procedures so that they can discuss and demonstrate their understanding during the problem-solving process. Demonstrating understanding is a process that must be continually practiced for students to be successful. Practice is especially important to help students apply their concrete, conceptual understanding during each step of the problem-solving process.

Understanding Assessment

In addition to providing opportunities for frequent practice, teachers must be able to assess students' problem-solving skills. This is important so that teachers can adequately address students' misconceptions, build on their current understandings, and challenge them appropriately. Assessment is a long-term process that involves careful analysis of student responses from discussions, projects, practice pages, or tests. When analyzing the data, it is important for teachers to reflect on how their teaching practices may have influenced students' responses and to identify those areas where additional instruction may be required. In short, the data gathered from assessments should be used to inform instruction: slow down, speed up, or reteach. This type of assessment is called *formative assessment*.

HOW TO USE THIS BOOK

180 Days of Problem Solving offers teachers and parents problem-solving activities for each day of the school year. Students will build their problem-solving skills as they develop a deeper understanding of mathematical concepts and apply these concepts to real-life situations. This series will also help students improve their critical-thinking and reasoning skills, use visual models when solving problems, approach problems in multiple ways, and solve multi-step, non-routine word problems.

Easy-to-Use and Standards-Based

These daily activities reinforce grade-level skills across a variety of mathematical concepts. Each day provides a full practice page, making the activities easy to prepare and implement as part of a classroom routine, at the beginning of each mathematics lesson as a warm-up or Problem of the Day, or as homework. Students can work on the practice pages independently or in cooperative groups. The practice pages can also be utilized as diagnostic tools, formative assessments, or summative assessments, which can direct differentiated small-group instruction during Mathematics Workshop.

Domains and Practice Standards

The chart below indicates the mathematics domains addressed and practice standards applied throughout this book. The subsequent chart shows the breakdown of which mathematics standard is covered in each week.

Note: Students may not have deep understanding of some topics in this book. Remember to assess students based on their problem-solving skills and not exclusively on their content knowledge.

Grade-Level Domains	Practice Standards
1. Operations and Algebraic Thinking 2. Number and Operations in Base Ten 3. Number and Operations—Fractions 4. Measurement and Data 5. Geometry	1. Make sense of problems and persevere in solving them. 2. Reason abstractly and quantitatively. 3. Construct viable arguments and critique the reasoning of others. 4. Model with mathematics. 5. Use appropriate tools strategically. 6. Attend to precision. 7. Look for and make use of structure. 8. Look for and express regularity in repeated reasoning.

HOW TO USE THIS BOOK (cont.)

College-and-Career Readiness Standards

Below is a list of mathematical standards that are addressed throughout this book. Each week students solve problems related to the same mathematical topic.

Week	Standard
1	Find the greatest common factor of two whole numbers less than or equal to 100.
2	Find the least common multiple of two whole numbers less than or equal to 12.
3	Use the distributive property to express a sum of two whole numbers 1–100 with a common factor as a multiple of a sum of two whole numbers with no common factor.
4	Fluently divide multi-digit numbers using the standard algorithm.
5	Interpret and compute quotients of fractions, and solve word problems involving division of fractions by fractions, e.g., by using visual fraction models and equations to represent the problem.
6	Fluently add, subtract, multiply, and divide multi-digit decimals using the standard algorithm for each operation.
7	Understand the concept of a ratio and use ratio language to describe a ratio relationship between two quantities.
8	Understand the concept of a unit rate $\frac{a}{b}$ associated with a ratio $a{:}b$ with $b \neq 0$, and use rate language in the context of a ratio relationship.
9	Make tables of equivalent ratios relating quantities with whole-number measurements, find missing values in the tables, and plot the pairs of values on the coordinate plane. Use tables to compare ratios.
10	Solve unit rate problems including those involving unit pricing and constant speed.
11	Find a percent of a quantity as a rate per 100 (e.g., 30% of a quantity means $\frac{30}{100}$ times the quantity); solve problems involving finding the whole, given a part and the percent.
12	Use ratio reasoning to convert measurement units; manipulate and transform units appropriately when multiplying or dividing quantities.
13	Understand that positive and negative numbers are used together to describe quantities having opposite directions or values (e.g., temperature above/below zero, elevation above/below sea level, credits/debits, positive/negative electric charge); use positive and negative numbers to represent quantities in real-world contexts, explaining the meaning of 0 in each situation.
14	Recognize opposite signs of numbers as indicating locations on opposite sides of 0 on the number line; recognize that the opposite of the opposite of a number is the number itself, e.g., $-(-3) = 3$, and that 0 is its own opposite. Find and position integers and other rational numbers on a horizontal or vertical number line diagram; find and position pairs of integers and other rational numbers on a coordinate plane.

HOW TO USE THIS BOOK *(cont.)*

15	Understand signs of numbers in ordered pairs as indicating locations in quadrants of the coordinate plane; recognize that when two ordered pairs differ only by signs, the locations of the points are related by reflections across one or both axes. Find and position integers and other rational numbers on a horizontal or vertical number line diagram; find and position pairs of integers and other rational numbers on a coordinate plane.
16	Interpret statements of inequality as statements about the relative position of two numbers on a number line diagram. Write, interpret, and explain statements of order for rational numbers in real-world contexts.
17	Understand the absolute value of a rational number as its distance from 0 on the number line; interpret absolute value as magnitude for a positive or negative quantity in a real-world situation. Distinguish comparisons of absolute value from statements about order.
18	Solve real-world and mathematical problems by graphing points in all four quadrants of the coordinate plane. Include use of coordinates and absolute value to find distances between points with the same first coordinate or the same second coordinate.
19	Draw polygons in the coordinate plane given coordinates for the vertices; use coordinates to find the length of a side joining points with the same first coordinate or the same second coordinate. Apply these techniques in the context of solving real-world and mathematical problems.
20	Write and evaluate numerical expressions involving whole-number exponents.
21	Write expressions that record operations with numbers and with letters standing for numbers. Identify parts of an expression using mathematical terms (sum, term, product, factor, quotient, coefficient); view one or more parts of an expression as a single entity. Evaluate expressions at specific values of their variables. Include expressions that arise from formulas used in real-world problems. Perform arithmetic operations, including those involving whole-number exponents, in the conventional order when there are no parentheses to specify a particular order (Order of Operations).
22	Apply the properties of operations to generate equivalent expressions. Identify when two expressions are equivalent (i.e., when the two expressions name the same number regardless of which value is substituted into them).
23	Understand solving an equation or inequality as a process of answering a question: which values from a specified set, if any, make the equation or inequality true? Use substitution to determine whether a given number in a specified set makes an equation or inequality true.
24	Use variables to represent numbers and write expressions when solving a real-world or mathematical problem; understand that a variable can represent an unknown number, or, depending on the purpose at hand, any number in a specified set.
25	Solve real-world and mathematical problems by writing and solving equations of the form $x + p = q$ and $px = q$ for cases in which p, q and x are all nonnegative rational numbers.

HOW TO USE THIS BOOK *(cont.)*

26	Write an inequality of the form $x > c$ or $x < c$ to represent a constraint or condition in a real-world or mathematical problem. Recognize that inequalities of the form $x > c$ or $x < c$ have infinitely many solutions; represent solutions of such inequalities on number line diagrams.
27	Use variables to represent two quantities in a real-world problem that change in relationship to one another; write an equation to express one quantity, thought of as the dependent variable, in terms of the other quantity, thought of as the independent variable. Analyze the relationship between the dependent and independent variables using graphs and tables, and relate these to the equation. For example, in a problem involving motion at constant speed, list and graph ordered pairs of distances and times, and write the equation $d = 65t$ to represent the relationship between distance and time.
28	Find the area of right triangles, other triangles, special quadrilaterals, and polygons by composing into rectangles or decomposing into triangles and other shapes; apply these techniques in the context of solving real-world and mathematical problems.
29	Find the volume of a right rectangular prism with fractional edge lengths by packing it with unit cubes of the appropriate unit fraction edge lengths, and show that the volume is the same as would be found by multiplying the edge lengths of the prism.
30	Apply the formulas $V = lwh$ and $V = bh$ to find volumes of right rectangular prisms with fractional edge lengths in the context of solving real-world and mathematical problems.
31	Represent three-dimensional figures using nets made up of rectangles and triangles, and use the nets to find the surface area of these figures. Apply these techniques in the context of solving real-world and mathematical problems.
32	Recognize a statistical question as one that anticipates variability in the data related to the question and accounts for it in the answers.
33	Understand that a set of data collected to answer a statistical question has a distribution, which can be described by its center, spread, and overall shape.
34	Recognize that a measure of center for a numerical data set summarizes all of its values with a single number, while a measure of variation describes how its values vary with a single number.
35	Display numerical data in plots on a number line, including dot plots, histograms, and box plots.
36	Report the number of observations. Describe the nature of the attribute under investigation, including how it was measured and its units of measurement. Give quantitative measures of center (median and/or mean) and variability (interquartile range and/or mean absolute deviation), as well as describe any overall pattern and any striking deviations from the overall pattern with reference to the context in which the data were gathered. Relate the choice of measures of center and variability to the shape of the data distribution and the context in which the data were gathered.

HOW TO USE THIS BOOK *(cont.)*

Using the Practice Pages

The activity pages provide practice and assessment opportunities for each day of the school year. Students focus on one grade-level skill each week. The five-day plan requires students to think about the problem-solving process, use visual models, choose multiple strategies, and solve multi-step, non-routine word problems. For this grade level, students may complete the pages independently or in cooperative groups. Teachers may prepare packets of weekly practice pages for the classroom or for homework.

Day 1–Think About It!
For the first day of each week, the focus is on thinking about the problem-solving process. Students might draw pictures or answer questions about a problem. The goal is to understand the process of solving a problem more so than finding the solution.

Day 2–Solve It!
On the second day of each week, students solve one to two routine problems based on the thinking process from Day 1. Students think about the information given in the problem, decide on a plan, solve the problem, and look back and explain their work.

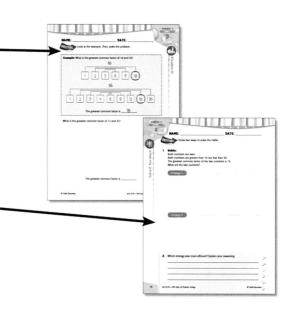

Day 3–Visualize It!
On day three, a visual representation (e.g., number line, table, diagram, fraction model) is shown as a strategy for solving a problem. Students use this visual model to solve a similar problem.

Day 4–Solve It Two Ways!
On the fourth day, students solve the same problem two ways by applying the strategies they have learned. Students may also be asked to analyze how others solved a problem and explain which way is correct or state the error or misconception.

HOW TO USE THIS BOOK *(cont.)*

Day 5–Challenge Yourself!
On day five, students are presented with a multi-step, non-routine problem. Students analyze a problem, think about different strategies, develop a plan, and explain how they solved the problem.

Using the Resources

The following resources will be helpful to students as they complete the activity pages. Print copies of these resources and provide them to students to keep at their desks. These resources are available as Adobe® PDFs online. A complete list of the available documents is provided on page 227. To access the digital resources, go to this website: **http://www.tcmpub.com/download-files**. Enter this code: 71758036. Follow the on-screen directions.

Practice Page Rubric can be found on page 219 and in the Digital Resources (rubric.pdf). The rubric can be used to assess students' mathematical understanding of the weekly concept and steps in the problem-solving process. The rubric should be shared with students so they know what is expected of them.

Problem-Solving Framework can be found on page 225 and in the Digital Resources (framework.pdf). Students can reference each step of the problem-solving process as they complete the practice pages during the week.

Problem-Solving Strategies can be found on page 226 and in the Digital Resources (strategies.pdf). Students may want to reference this page when choosing strategies as they solve problems throughout the week.

HOW TO USE THIS BOOK *(cont.)*

Diagnostic Assessment

Teachers can use the practice pages as diagnostic assessments. The data analysis tools included with the book enable teachers or parents to quickly score students' work and monitor their progress. Teachers and parents can quickly see which steps in the problem-solving process students need to target further to develop proficiency.

After students complete a week of practice pages, each page can be graded using the answer key (pages 193–218). Then, the *Practice Page Rubric* (page 219; rubric.pdf) can be used to score each practice page. The *Practice Page Item Analysis* (pages 220–223; itemanalysis.pdf) can be completed. The *Practice Page Item Analysis* can be used to record students' Day 5 practice page score, while the *Student Item Analysis* (page 224; studentitem.pdf) can be used to record a student's daily practice page score. These charts are also provided in the Digital Resources as PDFs, Microsoft Word® files (itemanalysis.docx; studentitem.docx), and Microsoft Excel® files (itemanalysis.xlsx; studentitem.xlsx). Teachers can input data into the electronic files directly on the computer, or they can print the pages and analyze students' work using paper and pencil.

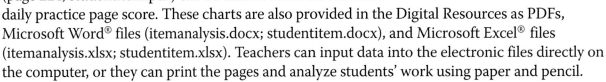

To Complete the Practice Page Item Analysis

- Write or type students' names in the far-left column. Depending on the number of students, more than one copy of the form may be needed, or you may need to add rows.

- The specific week is indicated across the top of each chart.

- Record rubric scores for the Day 5 practice page in the appropriate column.

- Add the scores for each student. Place that sum in the far-right column. Use these scores as benchmarks to determine how each student is performing after a nine-week period. This allows for four benchmarks during the year that can be used to gather formative diagnostic data.

HOW TO USE THIS BOOK *(cont.)*

To Complete the Student Item Analysis

- Write or type the student's name in the top row. This form tracks the ongoing process of each student, so one copy per student is necessary.

- The specific day is indicated across the top of each chart.

- Record the student's rubric score for each practice page in the appropriate column.

- Add the scores for the student. Place that sum in the far-right column. Use these scores as benchmarks to determine how the student is performing each week. These benchmarks can be used to gather formative diagnostic data.

Using the Results to Differentiate Instruction

Once results are gathered and analyzed, teachers can use the results to inform the way they differentiate instruction. The data can help determine which mathematical concepts and steps in the problem-solving process are the most difficult for students and which students need additional instructional support and continued practice.

Whole-Class Support

The results of the diagnostic analysis may show that the entire class is struggling with a particular mathematical concept or problem-solving step. If these concepts or problem-solving steps have been taught in the past, this indicates that further instruction or reteaching is necessary. If these concepts or steps have not been taught in the past, this data may indicate that students do not have a working knowledge of the concepts or steps. Thus, careful planning for the length of the unit(s) or lesson(s) must be considered, and additional front-loading may be required.

Small-Group or Individual Support

The results of the diagnostic analysis may show that an individual student or small group of students is struggling with a particular mathematical concept or problem-solving step. If these concepts or steps have been taught in the past, this indicates that further instruction or reteaching is necessary. These students can be pulled to a small group for further instruction on the concept(s) or step(s), while other students work independently. Students may also benefit from extra practice using games or computer-based resources. Teachers can also use the results to help identify individual students or groups of proficient students who are ready for enrichment or above-grade-level instruction. These groups may benefit from independent learning contracts or more challenging activities.

Digital Resources

The Digital Resources contain diagnostic pages and additional resources, such as the *Problem-Solving Framework* and *Problem-Solving Strategies* pages, for students. The list of resources in the Digital Resources can be found on page 227.

STANDARDS CORRELATIONS

Shell Education is committed to producing educational materials that are research- and standards-based. In this effort, we have correlated all of our products to the academic standards of all 50 states, the District of Columbia, the Department of Defense Dependents Schools, and all Canadian provinces.

How to Find Standards Correlations

To print a customized correlation report of this product for your state, visit our website at **http://www.tcmpub.com/shell-education**. If you require assistance in printing correlation reports, please contact our Customer Service Department at 1-877-777-3450.

Purpose and Intent of Standards

The Every Student Succeeds Act (ESSA) mandates that all states adopt challenging academic standards that help students meet the goal of college and career readiness. While many states already adopted academic standards prior to ESSA, the act continues to hold states accountable for detailed and comprehensive standards.

Standards are designed to focus instruction and guide adoption of curricula. Standards are statements that describe the criteria necessary for students to meet specific academic goals. They define the knowledge, skills, and content students should acquire at each level. Standards are also used to develop standardized tests to evaluate students' academic progress.

Teachers are required to demonstrate how their lessons meet state standards. State standards are used in the development of all of our products, so educators can be assured they meet the academic requirements of each state.

The activities in this book are aligned to today's national and state-specific college-and-career readiness standards. The chart on page 4 lists the domains and practice standards addressed throughout this book. A more detailed chart on pages 5–7 correlates the specific mathematics content standards to each week.

NAME: _____ **DATE:** _____

DIRECTIONS: Think about the problem, and answer the questions.

Gus's homework assignment is to find two numbers less than 50 with a greatest common factor of 8. He is not allowed to use 8 as one of the solution numbers. His solution pair is 16 and 32. Is Gus's solution correct?

1. What information do you know?

   _____

   _____

   _____

2. What do you need to find?

   _____

   _____

   _____

3. Why do you think Gus is not allowed to use 8 as a solution number?

   _____

   _____

   _____

NAME: _____ **DATE:** _____

DIRECTIONS: Read and solve the problem.

Solve It!

Problem: Gus's homework assignment is to find two numbers less than 50 with a greatest common factor of 8. He is not allowed to use 8 as one of the solution numbers. His solution pair is 16 and 32. Is Gus's solution correct?

 What Do You Know?

What Is Your Plan?

 Solve the Problem!

 Look Back and Explain!

NAME: _____ **DATE:** _____

DIRECTIONS: Look at the example. Then, solve the problem.

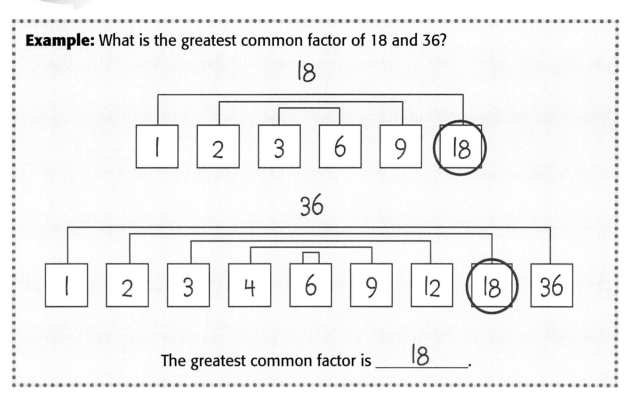

Example: What is the greatest common factor of 18 and 36?

The greatest common factor is ____18____.

What is the greatest common factor of 12 and 32?

The greatest common factor is _____.

Solve It Two Ways!

NAME: _____ DATE: _____

DIRECTIONS: Show two ways to solve the riddle.

1. **Riddle:**
   Both numbers are even.
   Both numbers are greater than 16 but less than 90.
   The greatest common factor of the two numbers is 16.
   What are the two numbers?

   Strategy 1

   Strategy 2

2. Which strategy was more efficient? Explain your reasoning.

_____

_____

_____

_____

#51618—180 Days of Problem Solving

NAME: _____ DATE: _____

DIRECTIONS: Read and solve the problem.

Jerome's Deli is preparing combination plates with at least one type of sandwich on each plate. There are 96 turkey club sandwiches, 64 ham and cheese sandwiches, and 32 meatball sandwiches. How many combination plates can the deli prepare if it wants the greatest number of plates possible, with the same number of sandwiches on each? How many of each type of sandwich will be on each combination plate?

Eat Ham!

Challenge Yourself!

1. Choose a strategy to show the number of combination plates.

2. Explain how you determined how many of each sandwich will be on each plate.

_____
_____
_____
_____
_____

Think About It!

NAME: _____ **DATE:** _____

DIRECTIONS: Think about the problem, and answer the questions.

Shelby likes to order the soup and sandwich daily special at the Fresh Lunch Café. There are 9 soups on the menu that repeat in the same order, with one soup served each day. There are 6 sandwiches that repeat in the same order, with one sandwich served each day. Today, the café is serving tomato soup with a grilled cheese sandwich. Shelby wants to know how many days it will take for the café to serve this same combination again.

1. What information do you know?

_____

_____

_____

2. What do you need to find?

_____

_____

_____

3. Shelby thinks that if she multiplies 9 and 6, she can find when the tomato soup with grilled cheese combination will be served again. Do you agree with Shelby's reasoning? Why or why not?

_____

_____

_____

_____

_____

NAME: _____ DATE: _____

 DIRECTIONS: Read and solve the problem.

Problem: Shelby likes to order the soup and sandwich daily special at the Fresh Lunch Café. There are 9 soups on the menu that repeat in the same order with one soup served each day. There are 6 sandwiches that repeat in the same order with one sandwich served each day. Today, the café is serving tomato soup with a grilled cheese sandwich. Shelby wants to know how many days it will take for the café to serve this same combination again.

 **What Do You Know?**

 What Is Your Plan?

Solve the Problem!

 Look Back and Explain!

Visualize It!

NAME: _____ **DATE:** _____

DIRECTIONS: Look at the example. Then, solve the problem using the ladder method.

Example: What is the least common multiple of 16 and 40?

multiples of 16: 16, 32, 48, 64, 80 96, 112...

multiples of 40: 40, 80 120...

The least common multiple is ____80____.

What is the least common multiple of 24 and 36?

The least common multiple is _____.

NAME: _____ DATE: _____

DIRECTIONS: Show two ways to solve the problem.

1. Denise has flute lessons every 4 days. Joshua has piano lessons every 10 days. They are both at music school today. In how many days will Denise and Joshua be together at music school again?

Strategy 1

Strategy 2

2. Which strategy do you think is more efficient? Explain your reasoning.

_____

_____

_____

_____

Challenge Yourself!

NAME: _____ **DATE:** _____

DIRECTIONS: Read and solve the problem.

A school nurse restocks bandages in packages of 12, sanitizing wipes in packages of 4, and tongue depressors in packages of 5. Last week, the nurse restocked the same number of bandages, sanitizing wipes, and tongue depressors. What is the least number of packages of each item that the nurse could have restocked?

1. Show how you found the least number of packages of each item.

2. Explain your reasoning for your answer.

_____

_____

_____

_____

_____

_____

NAME: _____ **DATE:** _____

 **DIRECTIONS:** Think about the problem, and answer the questions.

A grocery store manager receives a shipment of 30 tomatoes and 18 avocados. The manager wants to display the items next to each other in two rectangular arrays, using their greatest common factor as a common dimension. Use the greatest common factor to find the dimensions of each rectangular array. Then, use the distributive property to find the total number of items. Prove your answer by simplifying the expression.

1. What information do you know?

   _____

   _____

   _____

2. Why is the greatest common factor being used and not the least common multiple?

   _____

   _____

   _____

3. Ernesto thinks the greatest common factor of 30 and 18 is 3. Do you agree with Ernesto? Why or why not?

   _____

   _____

   _____

NAME: _____ **DATE:** _____

DIRECTIONS: Read and solve the problem.

Problem: The grocery store manager receives a shipment of 30 tomatoes and 18 avocados. The manager wants to display the items next to each other in two rectangular arrays, using their greatest common factor as a common dimension. Use the greatest common factor to find the dimensions of each rectangular array. Then, use the distributive property to find the total number of items. Prove your answer by simplifying the expression.

 What Do You Know?

 What Is Your Plan?

 Solve the Problem!

 Look Back and Explain!

NAME: _____ **DATE:** _____

DIRECTIONS: Look at the example. Then, solve the problem using an area model.

Example: Use the greatest common factor and distributive property to find the sum.

$21 + 35 = \boxed{}$

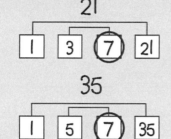

$(7 \times 3) + (7 \times 5) = 7(3 + 5)$

$21 + 35 = 7 \times 8$

$56 = 56$

GCF of 21 and 35 = ___7___

$21 + 35 =$ ___56___

Use the greatest common factor and distributive property to find the sum.

$18 + 81 = \boxed{}$

GCF of 18 and 81 = _____

$18 + 81 =$ _____

Solve It Two Ways!

NAME: _____ **DATE:** _____

DIRECTIONS: Show two ways to solve the problem.

1. A marching band director is arranging band members in a formation of two rectangular groups. One group has 54 marchers, and the other group has 66 marchers. The director wrote this formation as $(6 \times 9) + (6 \times 11)$. What are two other ways you can write this expression? Evaluate your expressions to check your work.

Expression 1 ·

Expression 2 ·

2. Which expression do you think shows the information in the best way? Explain your reasoning.

_____

_____

_____

NAME: _____ **DATE:** _____

DIRECTIONS: Read and solve the problem.

A library's parking lot is organized in an 8 × 9 rectangular array, partitioned into two smaller rectangular lots. Each lot holds a different number of vehicles. Neither lot holds fewer than 25 vehicles or more than 42 vehicles. What might be the dimensions of the smaller lots? Use the greatest common factor and distributive property to represent your solutions.

1. How many vehicles does the parking lot hold in total? Show your thinking.

2. Write two expressions to show how many vehicles are in the two smaller lots. Evaluate your expressions to check your work.

Think About It!

NAME: _____ DATE: _____

DIRECTIONS: Think about the problem, and answer the questions.

Lynn's teacher starts class by saying, "Today's your lucky day! I'm giving you the answer to a division problem. But, you must find the missing part of the problem." What is the missing number?

$$55\overline{)\,?} \quad \begin{array}{c} 143 \quad \text{r. } 6 \end{array}$$

1. What does "r. 6" represent?

_____

_____

_____

2. How many digits do you think the missing number has? Explain your reasoning.

_____

_____

_____

3. How can 143 and 55 help you find the missing number?

_____

_____

_____

NAME: _____ DATE: _____

 **DIRECTIONS:** Read and solve the problem.

Solve It!

Problem: Lynn's teacher starts class by saying, "Today's your lucky day! I'm giving you the answer to a division problem. But, you must find the missing part of the problem." What is the missing number?

$$55 \overline{)} \quad 143 \quad r.\ 6$$

? What Do You Know?

🔑 What Is Your Plan?

 Solve the Problem!

🔍 Look Back and Explain!

NAME: _____ DATE: _____

DIRECTIONS: Look at the example. Then, solve the problem.

Example: Use place value to explain each step of the division problem.

$$\begin{array}{r} 3 \\ 12\overline{)374} \\ -360 \\ \hline 14 \end{array}$$

There are ____30____ groups of 12 in 374.

____30____ × 12 = ____360____

374 – ____360____ = ____14____

$$\begin{array}{r} 31 \\ 12\overline{)374} \\ -360 \\ \hline 14 \\ -12 \\ \hline 2 \end{array}$$

There is ____1____ group of 12 in 14.

____1____ × 12 = ____12____

14 – ____12____ = ____2____

The remainder is ____2____.

Use place value to explain each step of the division problem.

$$\begin{array}{r} 1 \\ 42\overline{)538} \\ -420 \\ \hline 118 \end{array}$$

There are _____ groups of 42 in 538.

_____ × 42 = _____

538 – _____ = _____

$$\begin{array}{r} 12 \\ 42\overline{)538} \\ -420 \\ \hline 118 \\ -84 \\ \hline 34 \end{array}$$

There are _____ groups of 42 in 118.

_____ × 42 = _____

118 – _____ = _____

The remainder is _____.

#51618—180 Days of Problem Solving

NAME: _____ **DATE:** _____

DIRECTIONS: Show two ways to solve the problem.

1. Find two four-digit numbers that have a remainder of 3 when divided by 5. Prove your solutions.

> Solution 1 ·

> Solution 2 ·

2. What strategies did you use to find your solutions? What number patterns can help you solve the problem?

   _____

   _____

   _____

NAME: _____ **DATE:** _____

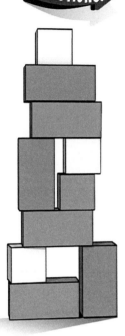

DIRECTIONS: Read and solve the problem.

Kami's little sister left her blocks scattered around the house. Kami knows there are between 100 and 150 blocks. After her sister picks up the blocks, she decides to play a game by arranging the blocks into equal stacks.

- When she arranges the blocks into 10 equal stacks, there are 4 left over.

- When she arranges the blocks into 11 equal stacks, there is 1 left over.

- When she arranges the blocks into 12 equal stacks, there are no blocks left over.

1. How many blocks does Kami's sister have? Prove your reasoning using words, numbers, or pictures.

2. What is another way Kami's sister can arrange her blocks into equal stacks so that there are no blocks left over? Explain your answer.

_____

_____

_____

NAME: _____ **DATE:** _____

DIRECTIONS: Think about the problem, and answer the questions.

One serving of salsa is $\frac{1}{16}$ of a pound. Alex uses $\frac{3}{4}$ of a pound of salsa to make a taco dip. How many servings of salsa are in the taco dip?

1. Is the question asking, "How many $\frac{1}{16}$s are in $\frac{3}{4}$?" or "How many $\frac{3}{4}$s are in $\frac{1}{16}$?" How do you know?

_____

_____

_____

_____

_____

2. Will the solution be less than or greater than one? How do you know?

_____

_____

_____

_____

_____

Solve It!

NAME: _____ **DATE:** _____

 DIRECTIONS: Read and solve the problem.

Problem: One serving of salsa is $\frac{1}{16}$ of a pound. Alex uses $\frac{3}{4}$ of a pound of salsa to make a taco dip. How many servings of salsa are in the taco dip?

? What Do You Know?

🔑 What Is Your Plan?

 Solve the Problem!

 Look Back and Explain!

NAME: _____ **DATE:** _____

DIRECTIONS: Look at the example. Then, solve the problem using the number line.

Visualize It!

Example: Lonnie has $1\frac{6}{10}$ meters of string to make friendship bracelets. Each bracelet requires $\frac{4}{5}$ meter of string. How many bracelets can she make?

$$1\frac{6}{10} \div \frac{4}{5} \qquad\qquad \frac{4}{5} = \frac{8}{10}$$

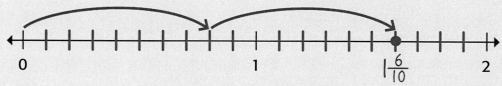

___2___ bracelets

Lonnie has $1\frac{1}{4}$ feet of twine to make friendship rings. Each ring requires $\frac{5}{12}$ foot of twine. How many rings can she make?

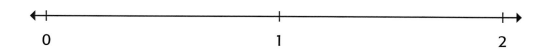

_____ rings

NAME: _____ DATE: _____

Solve It Two Ways!

DIRECTIONS: Show two ways to solve the problem.

1. Mr. Wells is making coffee in the teachers' lounge. Each pot of coffee requires $\frac{1}{6}$ pound of coffee. How many pots of coffee can he brew from a $2\frac{1}{2}$-pound bag of coffee?

Strategy 1

Strategy 2

2. Which strategy do you think is better? Explain your reasoning.

_____

_____

_____

_____

NAME: _____ **DATE:** _____

DIRECTIONS: Read and solve the problem.

Todd and Meredith enter a chili cook-off. One pot of chili requires $\frac{3}{8}$ cup of chicken stock and $\frac{1}{4}$ teaspoon cayenne pepper. Todd has $\frac{3}{8}$ cup of chicken stock and $\frac{5}{8}$ teaspoon of cayenne pepper. Meredith has $1\frac{1}{2}$ cups of chicken stock and $\frac{7}{8}$ teaspoon of cayenne pepper. If they combine their ingredients, how many pots of chili can they make?

1. How much of each ingredient do Todd and Meredith have altogether? Show your thinking.

2. Choose a strategy to solve the problem. Prove your reasoning using words, numbers, or pictures.

Think About It!

NAME: _____ DATE: _____

DIRECTIONS: Think about the problem, and answer the questions.

Dino walks along a path at the park. The distance of each section is shown in the diagram. How many meters does he walk from start to end? Estimate and then calculate the answer.

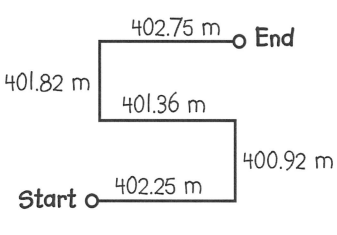

1. If Dino rounds to the nearest whole number, which of the following could be a list of his estimates for each section of the path?

   A. 402 + 400 + 401 + 401 + 402

   B. 403 + 401 + 402 + 402 + 403

   C. 402 + 401 + 401 + 402 + 403

2. Will the exact answer be less than or greater than 2,000 meters? How do you know?

   _____

   _____

   _____

   _____

   _____

NAME: _____ DATE: _____

 **DIRECTIONS:** Read and solve the problem.

Problem: Dino walks along a path at the park. The distance of each section of the path is shown in the diagram. How many meters does he walk from start to end? Estimate and then calculate the answer.

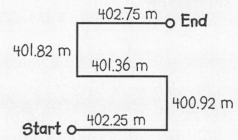

402.75 m o End
401.82 m
401.36 m
400.92 m
Start o 402.25 m

? What Do You Know?

🔑 What Is Your Plan?

💡 Solve the Problem!

🔍 Look Back and Explain!

Visualize It!

NAME: _____ DATE: _____

DIRECTIONS: Look at the example. Then, solve the problem.

Example: If $32 \times 58 = 1,856$, then what is the solution to each of these problems?

$$3.2 \times 58 = \underline{185.6}$$

$$3.2 \times 5.8 = \underline{18.56}$$

$$18.56 \div 5.8 = \underline{3.2}$$

$$185.6 \div 5.8 = \underline{32}$$

1. If $72 \times 14 = 1,008$, then what is the solution to each of these problems?

$$72 \times 1.4 = \underline{\hspace{2cm}}$$

$$7.2 \times 1.4 = \underline{\hspace{2cm}}$$

$$10.08 \div 1.4 = \underline{\hspace{2cm}}$$

$$100.8 \div 1.4 = \underline{\hspace{2cm}}$$

2. What patterns do you notice among the problems?

_____

_____

_____

_____

_____

_____

_____

_____

NAME: _____ **DATE:** _____

DIRECTIONS: Show two ways to solve the problem.

1. Wendy wants to visit an amusement park for her birthday. Admission is $95.00 per person. Her mom says that when she was Wendy's age, admission to the same park was only $5.25. How much will it cost for Wendy and one friend to go to the amusement park? How much would it have cost Wendy's mom and one friend when they were Wendy's age? How much more does it cost now for two people to go to the amusement park?

Strategy 1

Strategy 2

2. Which strategy do you think is more efficient? Explain your reasoning.

_____

_____

_____

_____

Challenge Yourself!

NAME: _____ **DATE:** _____

DIRECTIONS: Read and solve the problem.

The parent organization from West Middle School is buying lunch for the staff. The president has a $200 budget. She would like to buy some pies after buying everything else. How many pies will she be able to buy?

Food needed	Catering menu at the Fresh Lunch Café
1 pot of turkey chili	Pot of turkey chili. $18.50
2 pots of broccoli cheddar soup	Pot of broccoli cheddar soup . . . $12.25
1 sandwich assortment tray	Sandwich assortment tray $47.75
1 tray of Caesar salad	Tray of Caesar salad. $32.95
$\frac{1}{2}$ tray of chicken Caesar salad	Tray of chicken Caesar salad. . . . $37.80
_____ pies	Pie. $8.20

1. How much will the lunch cost without the pies? Show your thinking.

2. How many pies can the president of the parent organization buy? Explain your answer.

   _____

   _____

   _____

   _____

NAME: _____ DATE: _____

 DIRECTIONS: Think about the problem, and answer the questions.

Jackson orders glow-in-the-dark outer space wallpaper for his bedroom. The wallpaper has a repeating pattern of 1 planet surrounded by 4 shooting stars. Jackson wants to order more wallpaper. Since it is a special order, he needs to describe it accurately to the company. Draw a sketch of the pattern and name two ratios Jackson could use to describe the wallpaper.

1. Complete the statement: For every _____ planet, there are _____ shooting stars.

2. Label the following statements as accurate or inaccurate descriptions of Jackson's wallpaper. Explain your reasoning for each description.

   There are 4 shooting stars for every 1 planet.

   _____

   _____

   There are only 4 shooting stars in total on the wallpaper.

   _____

   _____

3. What are 3 ways you can write a ratio?

   _____

   _____

   _____

NAME: _____ **DATE:** _____

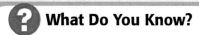 Read and solve the problem.

Solve It!

Problem: Jackson orders glow-in-the-dark outer space wallpaper for his bedroom. The wallpaper has a repeating pattern of 1 planet surrounded by 4 shooting stars. Jackson wants to order more wallpaper. Since it is a special order, he needs to describe it accurately to the company. Draw a sketch of the pattern and name two ratios Jackson could use to describe the wallpaper.

? What Do You Know?

** What Is Your Plan?**

** Solve the Problem!**

** Look Back and Explain!**

NAME: _____ DATE: _____

 DIRECTIONS: Look at the example. Then, solve the problem using a bar model.

Example: The ratio of koi fish to turtles in a pond is 7:4. There is a total of 55 koi fish and turtles in the pond. How many are koi fish? How many are turtles?

koi fish | 5 | 5 | 5 | 5 | 5 | 5 | 5

turtles | 5 | 5 | 5 | 5

There are ____55____ total animals. There are ____11____ squares.

____55____ ÷ ____11____ = ____5____

____7____ × ____5____ = ____35____

____4____ × ____5____ = ____20____

There are ____35____ koi fish and ____20____ turtles.

The ratio of cats to dogs at a pet store is 4:5. There are 108 cats and dogs at the pet store. How many are cats? How many are dogs?

There are _____ total animals. There are _____ squares.

_____ ÷ _____ = _____

_____ × _____ = _____

_____ × _____ = _____

There are _____ cats and _____ dogs.

NAME: _____ **DATE:** _____

DIRECTIONS: Show two ways to solve the problem.

1. On Saturday, Rise 'n' Shine Café sold 3 plain bagels for every 2 onion bagels. It sold 45 plain bagels. How many total bagels did the café sell?

Strategy 1

Strategy 2

2. Which strategy do you think is more efficient? Explain your reasoning.

_____

_____

_____

_____

NAME: _____ DATE: _____

DIRECTIONS: Read and solve the problem.

Bailey wants to make sparkling cranberry punch for her birthday party. She needs to combine cranberry juice, frozen pink lemonade concentrate, and club soda. The ratio of pink lemonade to club soda is 1 to 2. The ratio of pink lemonade to cranberry juice is 1:4. Bailey uses 64 ounces of cranberry juice. How many ounces of pink lemonade does she need? How many ounces of club soda does she need? How many total ounces of punch will there be?

1. Show how many ounces of pink lemonade concentrate Bailey will need.

2. Show how many ounces of club soda Bailey will need.

3. Explain how to find the total number of ounces of punch.

_____

_____

_____

NAME: _____ **DATE:** _____

DIRECTIONS: Think about the problem, and answer the questions.

Think About It!

A farmers' market sells 2 pints of blueberries for $5.00. How can you write a unit rate for this situation in two ways?

1. What information do you know?

_____

_____

_____

_____

2. What do you need to find?

_____

_____

_____

_____

3. What is the difference between a ratio and a unit rate?

_____

_____

_____

_____

_____

_____

_____

NAME: _____ DATE: _____

 DIRECTIONS: Read and solve each problem.

Solve It!

Problem 1: A farmers' market sells 2 pints of blueberries for $5.00. How can you write a unit rate for this situation in two ways?

 **What Do You Know?**

 What Is Your Plan?

 Solve the Problem!

 Look Back and Explain!

Problem 2: The farmers' market also sells 8 grapefruits for $12.00. How can you write a unit rate for this situation in two ways?

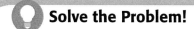 **What Do You Know?**

 What Is Your Plan?

 Solve the Problem!

 Look Back and Explain!

Visualize It!

NAME: _____ **DATE:** _____

DIRECTIONS: Look at the example. Then, solve the problem by completing the table.

Example: Carly walks 3 kilometers in 36 minutes on a treadmill. If she keeps this same pace, how long will it take her to walk 12 kilometers?

Minutes	12	24	36	72	120	144
Kilometers	1	2	3	6	10	12

__144__ minutes

Danielle takes 650 strides in 5 minutes on her elliptical machine. If she keeps this same pace, how long will it take her to complete 3,900 strides?

Minutes	1	2	4	5	10	15	
Strides		260	520	650	1,300	1,950	3,900

_____ minutes

NAME: _____ DATE: _____

DIRECTIONS: Show two ways to solve the problem.

1. A group of racehorses are running at a track. Chestnut runs 6 miles in 30 minutes. Beauty runs 4 miles in 10 minutes. Sunflower runs 1 mile in 15 minutes. Boots runs 10 miles in 20 minutes. Which horse runs the fastest?

Strategy 1

Strategy 2

2. Which strategy do you think is more efficient? Explain your reasoning.

_____

_____

_____

_____

Challenge Yourself!

NAME: _____ DATE: _____

DIRECTIONS: Read and solve the problem.

Valerie has three choices of Laundromats. All of them charge the same amount to wash a load of laundry, but the prices for drying a load are different.

- Sudsy Laundromat charges $0.25 for every 8 minutes of drying time.

- Fresh 'n' Dry Laundromat charges $0.10 for every 4 minutes of drying time.

- Squeaky Clean Laundromat charges $0.50 for every 10 minutes of drying time.

1. How many minutes of drying time does Sudsy Laundromat offer for $1.00? Show your thinking.

2. How many minutes of drying time does Fresh 'n' Dry Laundromat offer for $1.00? Show your thinking.

3. How many minutes of drying time does Squeaky Clean Laundromat offer for $1.00? Show your thinking.

4. Which Laundromat offers the best deal for drying a load of laundry? Explain your answer.

_____

_____

_____

NAME: _____ **DATE:** _____

 DIRECTIONS: Think about the problem, and answer the questions.

At Fresh Food grocery store, customers earn points for their purchases. The points are converted to "bonus bucks," which can be used to buy items at the store. One hundred Fresh Food points are worth $4.00 in "bonus bucks." If a customer uses $16.00 in "bonus bucks," how many points does he or she have?

Think About It!

1. What information do you know?

_____

_____

_____

2. What do you need to find?

_____

_____

_____

3. Is each point worth more or less than $1.00 in "bonus bucks"? How do you know?

_____

_____

_____

Solve It!

NAME: _____ **DATE:** _____

DIRECTIONS: Read and solve the problem.

Problem: At Fresh Food grocery store, customers earn points for their purchases. The points are converted to "bonus bucks," which can be used to buy items at the store. One hundred Fresh Food points are worth $4.00 in "bonus bucks." If a customer uses $16.00 in "bonus bucks," how many points does he or she have?

 What Do You Know?

 What Is Your Plan?

 Solve the Problem!

 Look Back and Explain!

NAME: _____ **DATE:** _____

DIRECTIONS: Look at the example. Then, solve the problem by using a rate table and a coordinate plane.

Example: A grocery store sells boxes of pasta. Four boxes cost $8.00. How much do 3 boxes cost? How many boxes can be purchased for $14.00?

Boxes of pasta	Cost (in dollars)
1	2
2	4
3	6
4	8
5	10
6	12
7	14
8	16

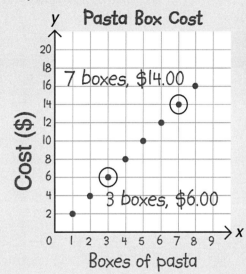

3 boxes cost ___$6.00___ and $14.00 will buy ___7___ boxes.

A store sells bottles of foaming hand soap. Six bottles cost $24.00. How much do 4 bottles cost? How many bottles of soap can be purchased for $40.00?

Bottles of soap	Cost (in dollars)
1	
2	
3	
4	
5	
6	24
7	
8	
9	
10	

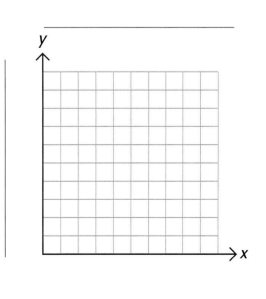

4 bottles of soap cost _____ and $40.00 will buy _____ bottles of soap.

NAME: _____ **DATE:** _____

DIRECTIONS: Show two ways to solve the problem.

1. Robin is a pet sitter. She feeds the dogs a mix of dry food and wet canned food. The ratio she uses is 3 scoops of dry food to 2 scoops of wet food. Using this ratio, how many scoops of dry food will Robin need for 16 scoops of wet food?

Strategy 1

Strategy 2

2. Which strategy do you think is more efficient? Explain your reasoning.

_____

_____

_____

_____

NAME: _____   DATE: _____

DIRECTIONS: Read and solve the problem.

Angela is shopping at the mall for a pair of jeans. She wants to find the best deal.

Pants Palace
2 jeans: $40

Denim Spot	
Pairs of jeans	**Price (in dollars)**
3	54
5	90
7	126

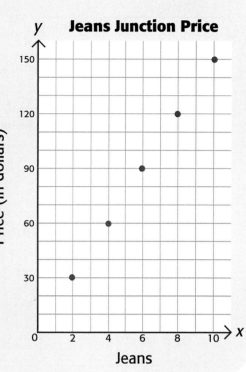

Jeans Junction Price

1. Which of the three stores is offering the lowest price? Which store has the highest price? Show your thinking.

2. Explain how you determined which store has the best deal.

_____

_____

_____

Think About It!

NAME: _____ **DATE:** _____

DIRECTIONS: Think about the problem, and answer the questions.

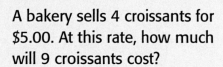

A bakery sells 4 croissants for $5.00. At this rate, how much will 9 croissants cost?

1. What information do you know?

_____

_____

_____

2. What do you need to find?

_____

_____

_____

3. Does each croissant cost more or less than $1.00? How do you know?

_____

_____

_____

4. Will the solution be more or less than $10.00? How do you know?

_____

_____

_____

NAME: _____ **DATE:** _____

 DIRECTIONS: Read and solve each problem.

Problem 1: A bakery sells 4 croissants for $5.00. At this rate, how much will 9 croissants cost?

 What Do You Know?

 What Is Your Plan?

 Solve the Problem!

 Look Back and Explain!

Problem 2: Bridget walks on her treadmill. She burns 55 calories every 5 minutes. At this rate, how many minutes does she need to walk to burn off a 220-calorie croissant?

 What Do You Know?

 What Is Your Plan?

 Solve the Problem!

 Look Back and Explain!

Visualize It!

NAME: _____ **DATE:** _____

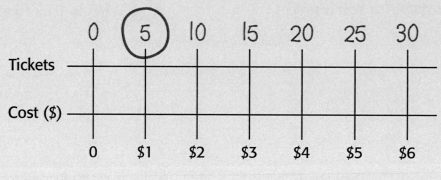

DIRECTIONS: Look at the example. Then, solve the problem using a double number line.

Example: Gabe wants to purchase ride tickets at the school carnival. The tickets are sold at a rate of 30 tickets for $6.00. How many tickets can Gabe purchase for $1.00?

Tickets   0   5   10   15   20   25   30

Cost ($)   0 $1 $2 $3 $4 $5 $6

Gabe can purchase ____5____ ride tickets for $1.00.

Gabe also wants to purchase food tickets to buy snacks. The food tickets are sold at a rate of 12 tickets for $3.00. How many food tickets can Gabe purchase for $1.00?

Tickets

Cost ($)   0 $1 $2 $3

Gabe can purchase _____ food tickets for $1.00.

NAME: _____ **DATE:** _____

DIRECTIONS: Show two ways to solve the problem.

1. Zoe's pet hamster can run a complete loop on a 24-inch exercise wheel in 3 seconds. At this rate, how many inches will the hamster run in 10 seconds?

Strategy 1

Strategy 2

2. Which strategy do you think is better? Explain your reasoning.

_____

_____

_____

_____

Challenge Yourself!

NAME: _____ DATE: _____

DIRECTIONS: Read and solve the problem.

Charlie and Charlotte are cheetahs that live in Africa. Charlie can run 90 meters in 10 seconds. Charlotte can run 110 meters in 11 seconds. Do the cheetahs run at the same speed?

1. How many meters per second can Charlie run? Show your thinking.

2. How many meters per second can Charlotte run? Show your thinking.

3. Explain how you solved the problem.

_____

_____

_____

_____

_____

NAME: _____ DATE: _____

 **DIRECTIONS:** Think about the problem, and answer the questions.

> Connor answers 17 out of 20 questions correctly on his math quiz. His teacher records all quiz grades as percentages. What percentage will Connor's teacher record for his math quiz?

Connor sets up the following table to find his percentage.

Correct answer	17	
Total	20	100

1. What information do you know?

_____

_____

_____

2. Why is Connor using 100 when there were not 100 questions on the quiz?

_____

_____

_____

3. Explain how the table will help Connor determine his percentage.

_____

_____

_____

Solve It!

NAME: _____ **DATE:** _____

 **DIRECTIONS:** Read and solve each problem.

Problem 1: Connor answers 17 out of 20 questions correctly on his math quiz. His teacher records all quiz grades as percentages. What percentage will Connor's teacher record for his math quiz?

 What Do You Know?

 What Is Your Plan?

 Solve the Problem!

 Look Back and Explain!

Problem 2: On his next math quiz, Connor answers 17 out of 25 questions correctly. What percentage will Connor's teacher record for this quiz? Is the percentage the same or different than his percentage on the quiz in question 1?

 What Do You Know?

 What Is Your Plan?

 Solve the Problem!

 Look Back and Explain!

NAME: _____ **DATE:** _____

 DIRECTIONS: Look at the example. Then, solve the problem using a bar model.

Visualize It!

Example: At Muir Academy, 40% of the students in sixth grade are members of the chorus. If there are 82 sixth graders in chorus, how many students are in sixth grade at Muir Academy?

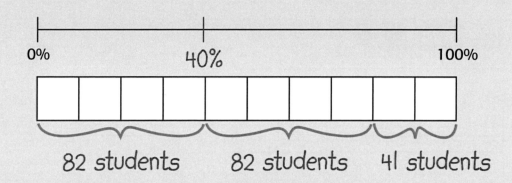

0%   40%   100%

82 students   82 students   41 students

82 + 82 + 41 = 205

There are 205 sixth graders at Muir Academy.

At Muir Academy, 30% of the students in seventh grade are members of the Science Explorers Club. If there are 78 seventh graders in the club, how many students are in seventh grade at Muir Academy?

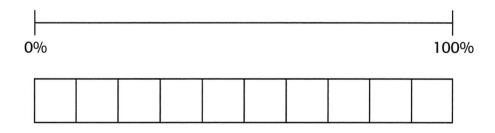

0%   100%

_____

_____

NAME: _____ DATE: _____

Solve It Two Ways!

DIRECTIONS: Show two ways to solve the problem.

1. Carla and Wes work in a bakery. They sell a one-dozen package of jumbo cookies. Carla and Wes decorate 75% of them with buttercream frosting. Complete Carla's and Wes's strategies to find how many cookies in each package need to be decorated with buttercream frosting.

Carla's Strategy

75	3	
100	4	12

Wes's Strategy

$$\frac{75}{100} \times 12 = \frac{\boxed{}}{\boxed{100}} = \boxed{} \text{ cookies}$$

2. Which strategy do you prefer? Explain your reasoning.

_____

_____

_____

_____

 #51618—180 Days of Problem Solving

NAME: _____ **DATE:** _____

DIRECTIONS: Read and solve the problem.

Caleb and his parents are celebrating his birthday. First, they visit his favorite restaurant for dinner. The bill is $55.00, and Caleb's parents add an 18% tip. Then, they buy Caleb new sneakers for $60.00, and they pay an additional 8% sales tax.

1. How much money do Caleb's parents spend on dinner, including the tip? Show your thinking.

2. How much money do his parents spend on the sneakers, including the sales tax? Show your thinking.

3. What is the total cost for his birthday celebration? Explain how you found your answer.

_____

_____

_____

_____

Think About It!

NAME: _____ **DATE:** _____

DIRECTIONS: Think about the problem, and answer the questions.

The door of Nicole's locker is 1 foot wide and 5 feet tall. She wants to decorate the inside of the door with pink zebra-striped paper. If there are 720 square inches of paper in the roll, how many square inches of paper will Nicole have left after she decorates her locker door?

Remember, 1 foot = 12 inches.

1. How wide is the door of Nicole's locker in inches? How tall is the door in inches?

    _____

    _____

    _____

2. Nicole thinks the area of the door of her locker is 5 square feet because 1 foot times 5 feet equals 5 square feet. She says the area of the paper is 720 square inches, and 720 minus 5 is 715, so she will have 715 square inches of paper left when she is finished. Do you agree with Nicole's reasoning? Why or why not?

    _____

    _____

    _____

    _____

    _____

NAME: _____ DATE: _____

 DIRECTIONS: Read and solve the problem.

Problem: The door of Nicole's school locker is 1 foot wide and 5 feet tall. She is decorating the entire inside of the door with pink zebra-striped paper. There are 720 square inches of paper in the roll. How many square inches of paper will Nicole have left after she decorates her locker door? Remember, 1 foot = 12 inches.

 What Do You Know?

 What Is Your Plan?

Solve the Problem!

Look Back and Explain!

NAME: _____ DATE: _____

Visualize It!

DIRECTIONS: Look at the example. Then, solve the problem by using a rate table.

Example: David is reading a book. A character in the book drives faster than the 80 kilometers per hour speed limit. David wonders if that is faster or slower than 60 miles per hour, like the highway near his house. Remember, 1 mile is approximately equal to 1.6 kilometers.

Kilometers (km)	1.6	16	96
Miles (mi.)	1	10	60

$1 \times 1.6 = 1.6$ $10 \times 1.6 = 16$ $60 \times 1.6 = 96$

Since 60 miles per hour is about 96 kilometers per hour, then 80 kilometers per hour is slower than 60 miles per hour.

Another character in David's book owns an English bulldog. The dog weighs 25 kilograms. David wonders if that is more or less than his golden retriever, which weighs 65 pounds. Remember, 1 kilogram is approximately equal to 2.2 pounds.

Pounds (lb.)	2.2		
Kilograms (kg)	1	10	25

_____

_____

_____

NAME: _____ **DATE:** _____

DIRECTIONS: Show two ways to solve the problem.

1. East Side Park measures 70 yards by 70 yards. The playground in the park, measures 90 feet by 90 feet. How much of the land at the park is **not** covered by the playground? Remember, 1 yard = 3 feet.

. . . . **Solution 1** . . . .

Find the solution in square feet.

. . . . **Solution 2** . . . .

Find the solution in square yards.

2. How are the solutions similar? How are the solutions different?

_____

_____

_____

_____

NAME: _____ **DATE:** _____

DIRECTIONS: Read and solve the problem.

Kaylie is excited about what happened at her equestrian center. She immediately emailed her friend Olivia, who lives in Canada.

> Dear Olivia,
>
> After a lot of fund-raising, the equestrian center finally has enough money to buy a new horse. He weighs 847 pounds and is 60 inches tall. I just had to share the exciting news!
>
> Your friend,
>
> Kaylie

Olivia wrote an email back to Kaylie.

> Hi Kaylie,
>
> That's great news about the new horse! But, I'm a little confused because in Canada, we use kilograms and centimeters. Can you help me convert these measurements? I found out there are about 2.2 pounds in 1 kilogram and about 2.54 centimeters in 1 inch.
>
> Thanks,
>
> Olivia

Write an email Kaylie can send to Olivia with the requested conversions.

_____

_____

_____

_____

_____

_____

NAME: _____ **DATE:** _____

 DIRECTIONS: Think about the problem, and answer the questions.

Carlos is the new treasurer of his school's student council. There are a few items he needs to record on the budget spreadsheet. What positive or negative number should Carlos use to represent each transaction?

- withdrawal of $30 for snacks at meetings

- donation of $50 from a community member

1. What important word(s) in the first item provide a clue as to whether to use a positive or negative number?

_____

_____

2. What important word(s) in the second item provide a clue as to whether to use a positive or negative number?

_____

_____

3. How do you know when to represent a situation with a positive or negative number?

_____

_____

_____

Solve It!

NAME: _____ **DATE:** _____

DIRECTIONS: Read and solve each problem.

Problem 1: Carlos is the new treasurer of his school's student council. There are a few items he needs to enter into the budget spreadsheet. What positive or negative number should Carlos use to represent each transaction?

- withdrawal of $30 for snacks at meetings
- donation of $50 from a community member

 What Do You Know?

 What Is Your Plan?

Solve the Problem!

Look Back and Explain!

Problem 2: The student council sells school pride T-shirts as a fund-raiser. What positive or negative number should Carlos use to represent each transaction?

- expenditure of $25 to print promotional flyers and order forms
- charge from the T-shirt company for $175 to print the T-shirts
- income of $500 from the fund-raiser

 What Do You Know?

 What Is Your Plan?

 Solve the Problem!

 Look Back and Explain!

NAME: _____ DATE: _____

 **DIRECTIONS:** Look at the example. Then, solve the problem by drawing a sketch.

Example: Some Mayan ruins in Mexico have a 25 ft. tall pyramid situated on the top of 40 ft. tall cliffs. The nearby sea has an average depth of 8,000 ft. How many feet higher is the top of the pyramid than the depth of the sea?

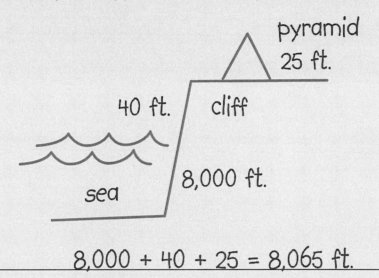

$$8,000 + 40 + 25 = 8,065 \text{ ft.}$$

A 455 ft. tall pyramid in Egypt is located near a town with an elevation of 223 ft. The nearby river has an average depth of 33 ft. How many feet higher is the top of the pyramid than the depth of the river?

_____

NAME: _____ **DATE:** _____

Solve It Two Ways!

DIRECTIONS: Show two ways to solve the problem.

1. Antonio is watching his favorite team play American football. The following is a list of several plays from the game. What is the team's overall yardage?

   - pass for a gain of 15 yards
   - rush for a gain of 5 yards
   - quarterback sack for a loss of 8 yards
   - fumble for a loss of 2 yards
   - quarterback sneak for a gain of 1 yard

   Strategy 1 ·

   Strategy 2 ·

2. Which strategy do you prefer? Explain your reasoning.

   _____

   _____

   _____

   _____

NAME: _____ **DATE:** _____

 **DIRECTIONS:** Read and solve the problem.

Students from North, South, East, and West Middle Schools are competing in a math competition. The questions vary in difficulty. Teams earn 10, 20, 30, 40, or 50 points for correct answers. However, teams lose those points if they give incorrect answers. The results after 5 rounds are shown in the tables below.

North Middle School		
Round	**Result**	**Points**
1	correct	10 points
2	correct	50 points
3	incorrect	30 points
4	correct	20 points
5	incorrect	40 points

South Middle School		
Round	**Result**	**Points**
1	incorrect	10 points
2	incorrect	20 points
3	correct	40 points
4	correct	30 points
5	correct	50 points

East Middle School		
Round	**Result**	**Points**
1	correct	50 points
2	correct	30 points
3	incorrect	10 points
4	correct	20 points
5	incorrect	40 points

West Middle School		
Round	**Result**	**Points**
1	incorrect	50 points
2	correct	20 points
3	incorrect	10 points
4	correct	40 points
5	correct	30 points

Rank the teams in order from first to last place. Show how to calculate each school's final score.

_____

Think About It!

NAME: _____ DATE: _____

DIRECTIONS: Think about the problem, and answer the questions.

Eva is in a parking garage elevator. She sees these buttons and labels:

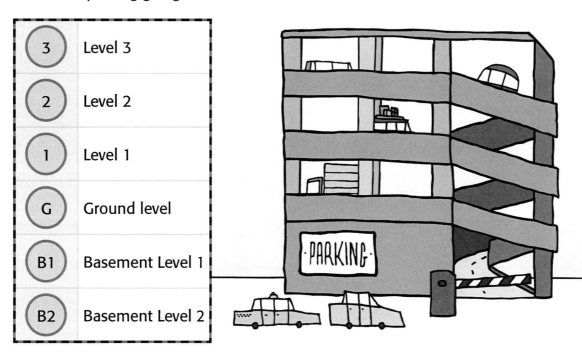

3	Level 3
2	Level 2
1	Level 1
G	Ground level
B1	Basement Level 1
B2	Basement Level 2

Eva is parked on Basement Level 2 and her friend Gabby is parked on Level 3. How many levels does Eva travel in the elevator to meet Gabby?

1. Is Eva starting above or below ground level?

_____

2. How can you represent Eva's original parking level with a positive or negative number?

_____

3. What level represents zero in this elevator? How do you know?

_____

_____

NAME: _____ **DATE:** _____

 DIRECTIONS: Read and solve the problem.

Solve It!

Problem: Eva is in a parking garage elevator. She sees these buttons and labels:

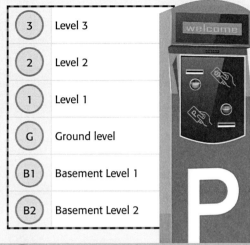

3	Level 3
2	Level 2
1	Level 1
G	Ground level
B1	Basement Level 1
B2	Basement Level 2

Eva is parked on Basement Level 2 and her friend Gabby is parked on Level 3. How many levels does Eva travel in the elevator to meet Gabby?

 What Do You Know?

 What Is Your Plan?

Solve the Problem!

Look Back and Explain!

Visualize It!

NAME: _____ **DATE:** _____

DIRECTIONS: Look at the example. Then, solve the problem using a number line.

Example: Write the opposite of each number in the table. Then, plot each number and its opposite on the number line.

Number	Opposite
−5	5
0.5	−0.5
$3\frac{1}{2}$	$-3\frac{1}{2}$
−1	1

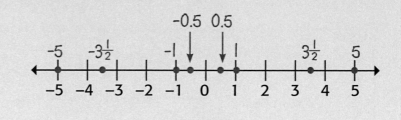

1. Write the opposite of each number in the table. Then, plot each number and its opposite on the number line.

Number	Opposite
$\frac{9}{2}$	
−2.5	
3	
$-1\frac{1}{3}$	

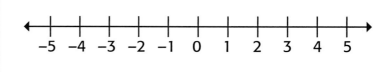

2. What do you notice about opposites and their distance from zero?

_____

_____

_____

_____

_____

_____

NAME: _____ **DATE:** _____

DIRECTIONS: Show two ways to solve the problem.

1. Kenny thinks the opposite of −4 is the same location as −(−4). Plot each number on a number line to determine if Kenny is correct.

Number line 1

Plot the opposite of −4.

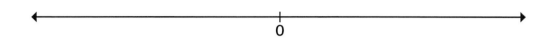

Number line 2

Plot −(−4).

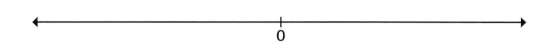

2. What do you notice about the points on the number lines? Explain your reasoning.

_____

_____

_____

_____

_____

_____

_____

Challenge Yourself!

NAME: _____ DATE: _____

DIRECTIONS: Read and solve the problem.

Grapey Goodness Raisin Company wants to put 30 raisins in each box. The quality control department tests boxes for accuracy. If there are exactly 30 raisins in a box, quality control enters a 0 into the computer. If the box contains more than 30 raisins, quality control enters a positive number to represent the excess number of raisins. If the box contains fewer than 30 raisins, quality control enters a negative number to represent the missing number of raisins.

The following are the results of ten inspections:

−5   +2   0   +3   +6   −6   −1   +4   −3   −2

1. Plot and label each result on the number line.

0

2. Any boxes that vary by more than 4 raisins need to be sent back to be repackaged. Use your number line to determine which boxes will need to be repackaged. Explain your reasoning.

_____

_____

_____

_____

_____

NAME: _____ DATE: _____

DIRECTIONS: Think about the problem, and answer the questions.

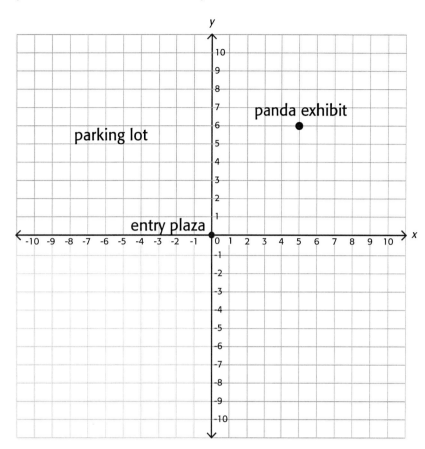

Wildlife Zoo is mapping its exhibits using a coordinate plane. The koala exhibit needs to be plotted as a reflection across the *x*-axis from the panda exhibit. What are the coordinates of the koala exhibit?

1. What is located at the origin (0, 0) of the coordinate plane?

_____

2. What does *reflection* mean?

_____

_____

3. In which quadrant is the panda exhibit located? _____

4. Andy thinks if he plots the koala exhibit as a reflection across the *x*-axis from the panda exhibit, it will be in the parking lot. Do you agree with Andy? Why or why not?

_____

_____

Solve It!

NAME: _____ DATE: _____

DIRECTIONS: Read and solve each problem.

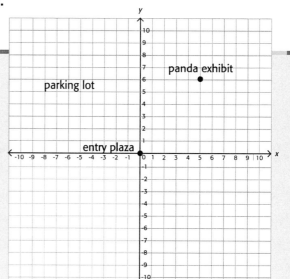

Problem 1: Wildlife Zoo is mapping its exhibits using a coordinate plane. The koala exhibit needs to be plotted as a reflection across the *x*-axis from the panda exhibit. What are the coordinates of the koala exhibit?

? **What Do You Know?**

🔑 **What Is Your Plan?**

💡 **Solve the Problem!**

🔍 **Look Back and Explain!**

Problem 2: The grizzly bear exhibit needs to be plotted as a reflection across the *y*-axis from the koala exhibit. What are the coordinates of the grizzly bear exhibit?

? **What Do You Know?**

🔑 **What Is Your Plan?**

💡 **Solve the Problem!**

🔍 **Look Back and Explain!**

NAME: _____ DATE: _____

DIRECTIONS: Look at the example. Then, solve the problem.

Example: Complete the table and plot the points on the coordinate plane.

Point	Coordinates
Point A	(−2, 4)
Point A reflected across the x-axis	(−2, −4)
Point A reflected across the y-axis	(2, 4)

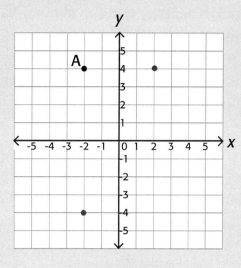

1. Complete the table and plot the points on the coordinate plane.

Point	Coordinates
Point B	
Point B reflected across the x-axis	
Point B reflected across the y-axis	

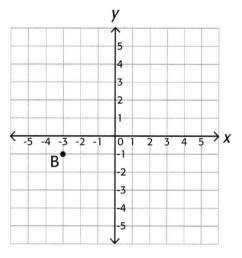

2. What do you notice about the coordinates of the original points and their reflections across the x-axis? What do you notice about the coordinates of the original points and their reflections across the y-axis?

_____

_____

_____

NAME: _____ **DATE:** _____

DIRECTIONS: Show two ways to solve the problem.

Solve It Two Ways!

1. Peter and Sophia want to write the x- and y-coordinates of the points shown on the coordinate plane. Peter writes the coordinates in a table. Sophia writes the coordinates as ordered pairs. Write the missing numbers in the table and ordered pairs.

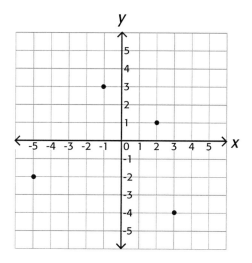

.... Peter's Strategy .... Sophia's Strategy ....

x	y
2	
	−4
−1	

(2, _____)

(_____ , −4)

(−1, _____)

(_____ , _____)

2. Which strategy do you think is better? Explain your thinking.

_____

_____

_____

_____

NAME: _____ DATE: _____

DIRECTIONS: Read and solve the problem.

Challenge Yourself!

Coastal Botanical Gardens is using a coordinate plane to plan the locations of the exhibits according to the following specifications:

- The rose garden must be at a point located in Quadrant II.
- The pine forest must be a point reflected across the *x*-axis from the rose garden.
- The herb garden must be a point reflected cross the *y*-axis from the pine forest.
- The aquatic plant pond must be a point located directly on the *x*-axis, between Quadrants II and III.
- The refreshment stand must be a point located directly on the *y*-axis, between Quadrants III and IV.
- The parking lot will be located in the quadrant that is empty.

Use the specifications to plot a point and label each location on the coordinate plane. Write the coordinates for each location in the table.

Exhibit	Coordinates
rose garden	
pine forest	
herb garden	
aquatic plant pond	
refreshment stand	
parking lot	Quadrant _____

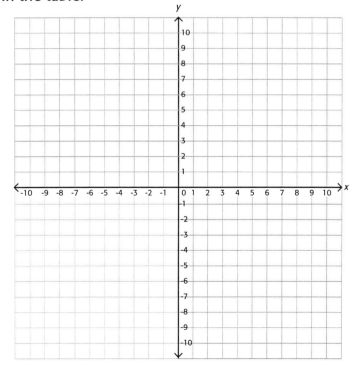

Think About It!

NAME: _____ **DATE:** _____

DIRECTIONS: Think about the problem, and answer the questions.

At the city library, the fines for overdue materials show up on the borrower's account as a negative amount. The fine for overdue books is $0.10 per day, and the fine for overdue games and DVDs is $0.20 per day. Theo has a book that is 4 days overdue and a game that is 2 days overdue. Joy has a book that is 5 days overdue and a DVD that is 1 day overdue. Who owes the library more money? Write an inequality to compare Theo's fines to Joy's fines. Use negative numbers to represent the amounts they owe.

1. Theo thinks he and Joy owe the same amount because their materials are both 6 days overdue. Do you agree with Theo's reasoning?

   _____

   _____

   _____

2. Do you think Theo owes more than $1.00? Does Joy owe more than $1.00? How do you know?

   _____

   _____

   _____

3. Why do you think the library keeps track of fees in negative amounts?

   _____

   _____

   _____

NAME: _____ **DATE:** _____

 DIRECTIONS: Read and solve the problem.

Problem: At the city library, the fines for overdue materials show up on the borrower's account as a negative amount. The fine for overdue books is $0.10 per day, and the fine for overdue games and DVDs is $0.20 per day. Theo has a book that is 4 days overdue and a game that is 2 days overdue. Joy has a book that is 5 days overdue and a DVD that is 1 day overdue. Who owes the library more money? Write an inequality to compare Theo's fines to Joy's fines. Use negative numbers to represent the amounts they owe.

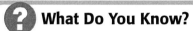 **What Do You Know?**

 What Is Your Plan?

Solve the Problem!

 **Look Back and Explain!**

Visualize It!

NAME: _____ DATE: _____

DIRECTIONS: Look at the example. Then, solve the problem using the thermometers to make comparisons.

Example: The low temperature in January in International Falls, Minnesota, is −21°C. The low temperature in January in Minneapolis, Minnesota, is −14°C. Shade the thermometers to show the low temperatures for each city. Write an inequality to compare the temperatures. How many degrees colder is the lower temperature?

International Falls   Minneapolis

−21 < −14

The low temperature in International Falls was colder than in Minneapolis by 7°C.

The low temperature in March in Billings, Montana, is −3°C. The low temperature in March in Lewistown, Montana, is −6°C. Shade the thermometers to show the low temperatures for each city. Write an inequality to compare the temperatures. How many degrees colder is the lower temperature?

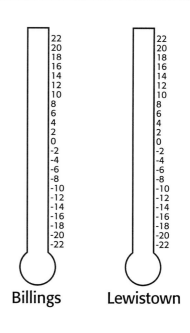

Billings   Lewistown

_____

_____

_____

NAME: _____ DATE: _____

DIRECTIONS: Show two ways to solve the problem.

1. Janisa purchases a parakeet from a pet store. She keeps track of how much weight, in ounces, the parakeet gains and loses to monitor his health. Janisa makes this list:

$$+\frac{3}{8} \qquad -\frac{3}{4} \qquad +\frac{1}{2} \qquad -\frac{15}{16}$$

Plot the weight gains or losses on the number line.

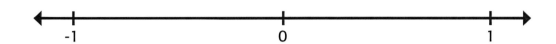

In each set, circle the correct inequality that Janisa can report to the veterinarian to show the parakeet's greatest weight gain or loss.

Set 1

$$\frac{1}{2} > \frac{3}{8} \qquad \text{or} \qquad \frac{1}{2} < \frac{3}{8}$$

Set 2

$$-\frac{3}{4} > -\frac{15}{16} \qquad \text{or} \qquad -\frac{3}{4} < -\frac{15}{16}$$

2. How does plotting numbers on a number line help you to compare them?

_____

_____

_____

_____

_____

NAME: _____ DATE: _____

DIRECTIONS: Read and solve the problem.

A meteorologist in Saskatchewan, Canada, is monitoring daily temperatures. She wants to rank the temperatures, in degrees Celsius, for the last two weeks in February from coldest to warmest.

Week 1	−3	−7	−6	−9	−2	5	0
Week 2	−11	−13	−5	3	−1	1	2

1. Rank the temperatures from coldest to warmest.

_____ , _____ , _____ , _____ , _____ ,

_____ , _____ , _____ , _____ , _____ ,

_____ , _____ , _____ , _____

2. Use your ordered list to plot and label the temperatures on the number line.

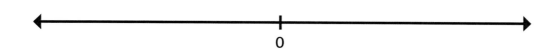

0

3. Determine how many days had temperatures above 0°C and how many days had temperatures below 0°C.

_____

_____

NAME: _____ **DATE:** _____

 DIRECTIONS: Think about the problem, and answer the questions.

In January, the temperature in Fargo, North Dakota, was −2°F. On the same day, the temperature in Cheyenne, Wyoming, was 1°F. Write an inequality to compare the temperatures. Then, write an inequality to compare the absolute values of the temperatures.

JANUARY

SUN	MON	TUE	WED	THU	FRI	SAT
1	2	3	4	5	6	7
8	9	10	11	12	13	14
15	16	17	18	19	20	21
22	23	24	25	26	27	28
29	30	31				

Think About It!

1. What information do you know?

_____

_____

_____

2. What does *absolute value* mean?

_____

_____

_____

3. Stephen writes 2 > −1 when writing the inequality for the absolute value of the temperatures. Should his teacher mark his answer correct or incorrect? Explain your reasoning.

_____

_____

_____

NAME: _____ DATE: _____

 DIRECTIONS: Read and solve each problem.

Solve It!

Problem 1: In January, the temperature in Fargo, North Dakota, was −2°F. On the same day, the temperature in Cheyenne, Wyoming, was 1°F. Write an inequality to compare the temperatures. Then, write an inequality to compare the absolute values of the temperatures.

? What Do You Know?

🔑 What Is Your Plan?

💡 Solve the Problem!

🔍 Look Back and Explain!

Problem 2: In January, the temperature in Caribou, Maine, was −9°F. On the same day, the temperature in Gunnison, Colorado, was −7°F. Write an inequality to compare the temperatures. Then, write an inequality to compare the absolute values of the temperatures.

? What Do You Know?

🔑 What Is Your Plan?

💡 Solve the Problem!

🔍 Look Back and Explain!

NAME: _____ **DATE:** _____

DIRECTIONS: Look at the example. Then, solve the problem.

Example: At the state fair frog-jumping contest, all frogs start at 0 on a line and take one jump. Their distance from 0 is their score. A frog earns a score of 3. Where might the frog have landed on the number line? Write an absolute value statement to show your answer.

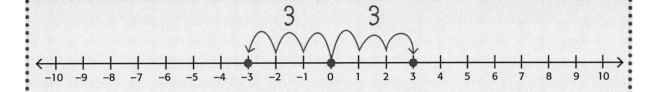

The frog may have landed on −3 or 3. Both −3 and 3 are 3 spaces away from 0 on the number line.

|−3| and |3| is 3.

A frog earns a score of 7. Where might the frog have landed on the number line? Write an absolute value statement to show your answer.

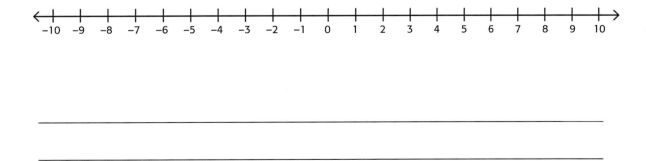

_____

_____

_____

Solve It Two Ways!

NAME: _____ DATE: _____

DIRECTIONS: Solve each set of comparisons.

1. James has a new video game. To win, he has to complete a maze before the time runs out. His score is reported as a positive number to show how much time he is over, or a negative number to show how much time he is under. His first four scores were 1:30, –0:45, –1:45, and 1:05.

Set 1

Which score is closest to the time allotment?

_____

Which score is farthest from the time allotment?

_____

Set 2

Which score has the least absolute value?

_____

Which score has the greatest absolute value?

_____

2. What do the two sets have in common?

_____

_____

_____

_____

NAME: _____ DATE: _____

 DIRECTIONS: Read and solve the problem.

Many animals can dive and soar several feet above and below sea level. Sea level has an elevation of 0 ft. Show how far each animal is from sea level.

1. Complete the table by writing the distance in absolute value notation and find the absolute value.

Animal	Distance from sea level	Absolute value notation	Absolute value
hammerhead shark	260 ft. below sea level	|−260|	260
California condor	15,000 ft. above sea level		
anglerfish	3,000 ft. below sea level		
pelican	9,000 ft. above sea level		
emperor penguin	900 ft. below sea level		
Mexican free-tailed bat	600 ft. above sea level		
dolphin	290 ft. below sea level		
peregrine falcon	3,000 ft. above sea level		

2. Place the animals in order from greatest distance from sea level to least distance from sea level.

_____ , _____ , _____ , _____ ,

_____ , _____ , _____ , _____

Challenge Yourself!

NAME: _____ **DATE:** _____

Think About It!

DIRECTIONS: Think about the problem, and answer the questions.

Snack and Save grocery store is organized using a coordinate-plane system. If each unit is 1 yard, what is the distance between the cereal and the milk?

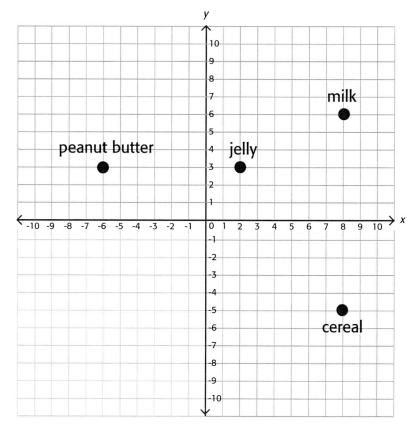

1. How can you find the location of the cereal?

   _____

   _____

2. How can you find the location of the milk?

   _____

   _____

3. If you connect the points for cereal and milk, does it create a vertical or horizontal line? What do all of the points on the line have in common?

   _____

   _____

   _____

NAME: _____ **DATE:** _____

DIRECTIONS: Read and solve each problem.

Solve It!

Problem 1: Snack and Save grocery store is organized using a coordinate plane system. If each unit is 1 yard, what is the distance between the cereal and the milk?

Coordinate plane showing: peanut butter at (-6, 4), jelly at (2, 3), milk at (8, 6), cereal at (8, -5)

? **What Do You Know?**

⚷ **What Is Your Plan?**

💡 **Solve the Problem!**

🔍 **Look Back and Explain!**

Problem 2: Looking at the coordinate plane in problem 1, what is the distance between the peanut butter and jelly?

? **What Do You Know?**

⚷ **What Is Your Plan?**

💡 **Solve the Problem!**

🔍 **Look Back and Explain!**

Visualize It!

NAME: _____ **DATE:** _____

DIRECTIONS: Look at the example. Then, solve the problem using a coordinate plane and number line.

Example: Sixth graders are planning a treasure hunt for a kindergarten class. They use a coordinate-plane system to hide the prizes on a field. What is the distance between Prize A and Prize B?

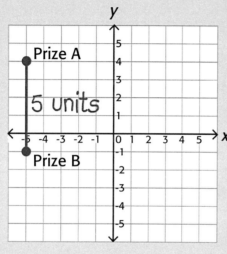

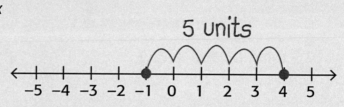

The distance between Prize A and Prize B is _____5_____ units.

What is the distance between Prize C and Prize D?

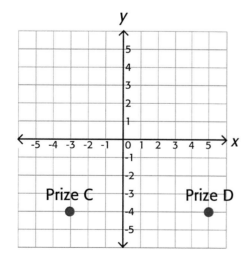

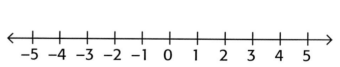

The distance between Prize C and Prize D is _____ units.

NAME: _____ DATE: _____

 DIRECTIONS: Show two ways to solve the problem.

1. An amusement park is organized using a coordinate-plane system. The Rocket Roller Coaster is located at $(8\frac{1}{2}, -2)$. The Kiddie Minicoaster is located at $(-7\frac{1}{4}, -2)$. What is the distance between the Rocket Roller Coaster and the Kiddie Minicoaster?

Strategy 1

Plot and label the points for each roller coaster on the coordinate plane. Then, count the spaces to find the distance.

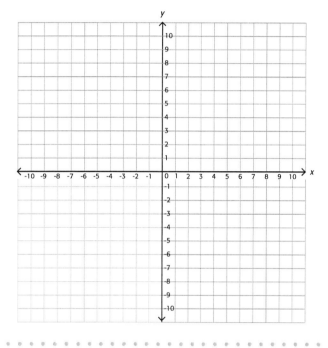

Strategy 2

2. Which strategy do you think is more efficient? Explain your reasoning.

_____

_____

_____

NAME: _____ DATE: _____

Challenge Yourself!

DIRECTIONS: Read and solve the problem.

Some people enjoy riding roller coasters. Other people don't. The difference in opinion often has to do with the difference between the highest and lowest hills on a coaster. Adventure World amusement park has eight coasters. The coordinate graph shows the height, in feet, of each coaster's highest and lowest hills.

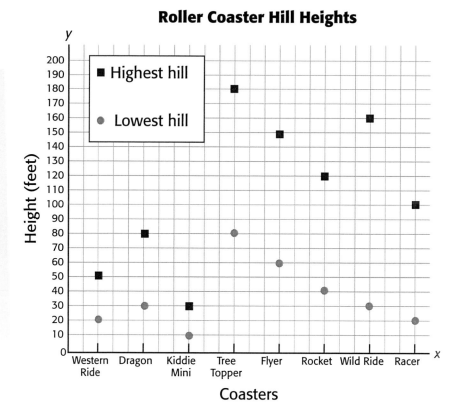

Roller Coaster Hill Heights

1. What is the difference between the heights of the highest and lowest hills for each coaster?

2. Put the coasters in order from greatest difference to least difference.

_____ , _____ , _____ , _____ ,

_____ , _____ , _____ , _____

NAME: _____ **DATE:** _____

 DIRECTIONS: Think about the problem, and answer the questions.

> Maya designs custom T-shirts. She plots her designs on a coordinate plane before transferring them to the shirts. She plots the following points and uses line segments to connect them in order: (8, 0), (5, 5), (–5, 5), (–8, 0), (–5, –5), and (5, –5). She connects the last point back to the first point. Plot the points to find what geometric shape Maya designed.

1. How many points does Maya plot? How do you know?

_____

_____

_____

2. What does the number of points tell you about the sides and vertices of the shape?

_____

_____

_____

3. Why do you think Maya plots her designs on a coordinate plane before putting them on T-shirts?

_____

_____

_____

NAME: _____ **DATE:** _____

DIRECTIONS: Read and solve each problem.

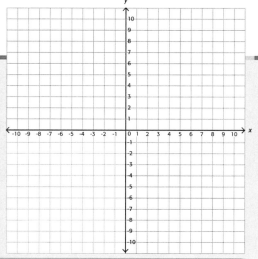

Problem 1: Maya designs custom T-shirts. She plots her designs on a coordinate plane before transferring them to the shirts. She plots the following points and uses line segments to connect them in order: (8, 0), (5, 5), (−5, 5), (−8, 0), (−5, −5), and (5, −5). She connects the last point back to the first point. Plot the points to find what geometric shape Maya designed.

 **What Do You Know?**

What Is Your Plan?

 Solve the Problem!

Look Back and Explain!

Problem 2: For her next design, Maya plots the following points and connects them in order: (0, 5), (−3, 2), (−3, 0), (3, 0), and (3, 2). She connects the last point back to her first point. Plot Maya's points on the same coordinate plane in problem 1 to find what geometric shape she designs.

 What Do You Know?

What Is Your Plan?

 Solve the Problem!

Look Back and Explain!

NAME: _____ DATE: _____

 DIRECTIONS: Look at the example. Then, solve the problem.

Example: If the points (4, 2), (−1, 2), and (−1, −3) are three vertices of a square, what are the coordinates of the final vertex? What is the length of each side of the square? Plot and label the points on the coordinate plane.

(__4__ , __−3__)

Each side of the square is ___5___ units long.

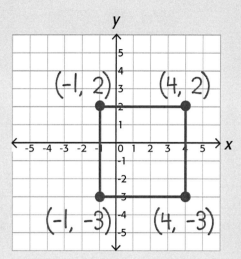

Visualize It!

If the points (5, 1), (−2, 1), and (−2, −2) are three vertices of a rectangle, what are the coordinates of the final vertex? What are the lengths of each side of the rectangle? Plot and label the points on the coordinate plane.

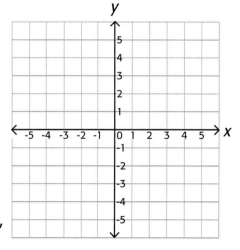

(_____ , _____)

Two sides of the rectangle are _____ units long,

and two sides are _____ units long.

Solve It Two Ways!

NAME: _____ **DATE:** _____

DIRECTIONS: Show two ways to solve the problem.

1. Use the vertices plotted on the coordinate planes to sketch two different rectangles. Plot and label the additional vertices needed and find the length of each side.

Rectangle 1

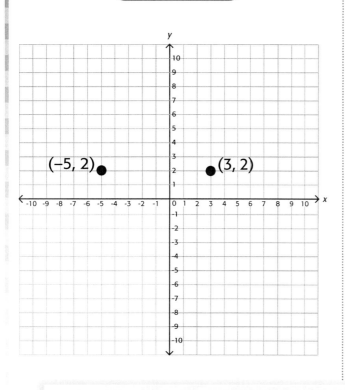

Rectangle 2

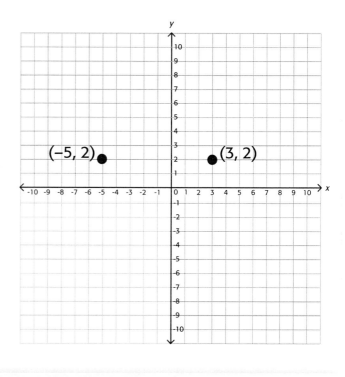

2. What is similar about the rectangles? What is different about the rectangles?

_____

_____

_____

_____

_____

_____

_____

NAME: _____ DATE: _____

DIRECTIONS: Read and solve the problem.

Sixth graders at Franklin Middle School are going to science camp. They are designing their cabin flags using a coordinate plane. Each unit on the coordinate plane represents 1 foot. Each flag must use the points (−3, 3) and (−3, −3) as vertices. One cabin's flag is a square. The other cabin's flag is a rectangle.

Finish designing each cabin's flag. Plot and label the coordinates you used. Find the length of each side to prove your designs are a square and a rectangle.

Square Flag

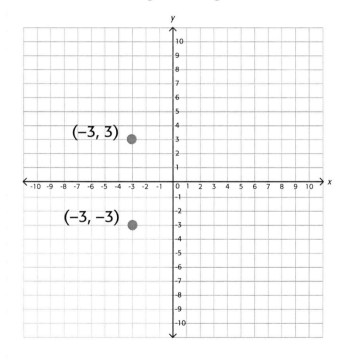

Rectangle Flag

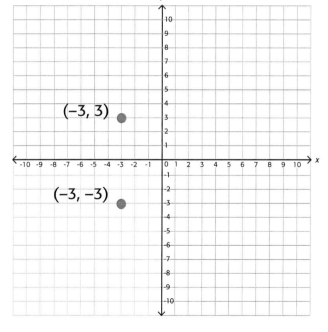

Think About It!

NAME: _____ **DATE:** _____

DIRECTIONS: Think about the problem, and answer the questions.

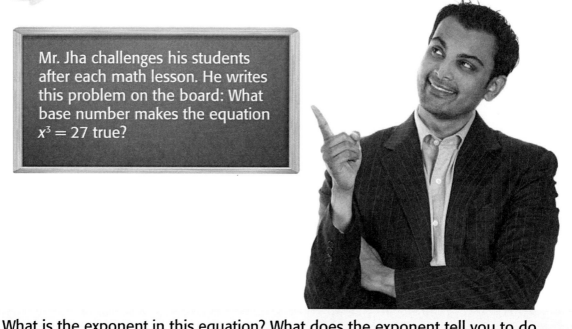

Mr. Jha challenges his students after each math lesson. He writes this problem on the board: What base number makes the equation $x^3 = 27$ true?

1. What is the exponent in this equation? What does the exponent tell you to do to the base?

_____

_____

_____

2. What is x^3 in expanded form?

_____

3. Isabel thinks the base number must be 9 because 9 × 3 is 27. Do you agree with her reasoning? Why or why not?

_____

_____

_____

_____

_____

_____

_____

NAME: _____ DATE: _____

 **DIRECTIONS:** Read and solve each problem.

Problem 1: Mr. Jha challenges his students after each math lesson. He writes this problem on the board: What base number makes the equation $x^3 = 27$ true?

 What Do You Know?

 What Is Your Plan?

 Solve the Problem!

 Look Back and Explain!

Problem 2: The next day, Mr. Jha gives his students another challenge problem: What exponent makes the equation $3^x = 81$ true?

 What Do You Know?

 What Is Your Plan?

 Solve the Problem!

 Look Back and Explain!

NAME: _____ **DATE:** _____

Visualize It!

DIRECTIONS: Look at the example. Then, solve the problem by drawing a diagram.

Example: Find the area of a rectangle with a width of x and a length 4 times its width.

x [rectangle]
4x

Area = $l \cdot x$

$A = 4x \cdot x$

$A = 4x^2$

If $x = 2$, what is the area of the rectangle?

$\underline{A = 4 \cdot 2^2 = 4 \cdot 4 = 16 \text{ square units}}$

Find the area of a square with side lengths of $6x$.

If $x = \frac{1}{3}$, what is the area of the square?

_____

NAME: _____ DATE: _____

DIRECTIONS: Show two ways to solve the problem.

1. Write two expressions that equal 24. Use at least one exponent in each expression. Evaluate your expressions to prove they equal 24.

> Expression 1 ·

> Expression 2 ·

Solve It Two Ways!

2. How did you decide what base numbers and exponents to use when writing your expressions?

_____

_____

_____

_____

NAME: _____ DATE: _____

DIRECTIONS: Read and solve the problem.

Melissa is a microbiologist. In the morning, she studies a sample of 5 bacteria. The bacteria sample doubles every hour. How many bacteria will there be after Melissa's eight-hour workday?

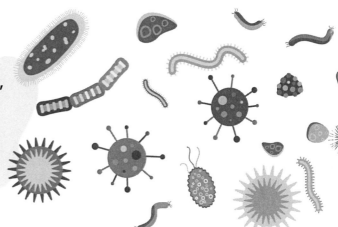

Challenge Yourself!

1. Write an expression with an exponent to represent the problem.

2. Evaluate your expression to solve the problem.

3. If Melissa works a 10-hour workday, how does the expression change? Write and evaluate the new expression to solve the problem.

4. If the sample triples every hour, how does the original expression change? Write and evaluate the new expression to solve the problem.

NAME: _____ DATE: _____

 DIRECTIONS: Think about the problem, and answer the questions.

> Cory tutors students in math. He charges a onetime fee of $15 for his lesson preparation, and then $12 per hour. Write an expression to show Cory's tutoring charges for any number of hours (h). Then, use the expression to find out how much money Cory will make by tutoring a student for 6 hours.

1. What variable will be used in the expression? What does it represent?

   _____

   _____

2. Cory's friend Laura thinks that Cory can add 15 and 12 to get 27. Then, he can multiply the number of hours he tutors by 27. Do you agree with Laura's reasoning? Why or why not?

   _____

   _____

   _____

3. What operations do you think Cory will use in the expression? Explain your answer.

   _____

   _____

   _____

NAME: _____ DATE: _____

Read and solve each problem.

Solve It!

Problem 1: Cory tutors students in math. He charges a onetime fee of $15 for his lesson preparation, and then $12 per hour. Write an expression to show Cory's tutoring charges for any number of hours (*h*). Then, use the expression to find out how much money Cory will make by tutoring a student for 6 hours.

 What Do You Know?

 What Is Your Plan?

 Solve the Problem!

 Look Back and Explain!

Problem 2: Cory needs to buy materials for the sixth-grade students he tutors. He buys a sixth-grade teacher's guide, which costs $18.50. He also buys an $8.50 workbook for each student in his tutoring group. Write an expression to show how much Cory will spend in materials for any number of students (*s*). Then, use the expression to find the total cost of materials for 4 students.

 What Do You Know?

 What Is Your Plan?

 Solve the Problem!

 Look Back and Explain!

NAME: _____ DATE: _____

 DIRECTIONS: Look at the example. Then, solve the problem by completing the table.

Visualize It!

Example: Write the missing phrase or algebraic expression.

Phrase	Algebraic Expression
the sum of a number and 7	$n + 7$
the quotient of 7 and a number	$\dfrac{7}{n}$
7 less than a number	$n - 7$
the difference of 7 and a number	$7 - n$
the product of 7 and a number	$7n$

Write the missing phrase or algebraic expression.

Phrase	Algebraic Expression
8 more than the product of 5 and a number	
	$\dfrac{4}{n} - 10$
Four times the difference of a number and 6	
	$3(9 + n)$
	$\dfrac{n}{2}$
2 less than the product of 11 and a number	

NAME: _____ **DATE:** _____

DIRECTIONS: Show two ways to solve the problem.

Solve It Two Ways!

1. Jamal and his friends go to a movie. Each person buys a movie ticket and a popcorn, candy, and drink combo. Tickets are $7.50 each. Combos are $12.00 each. Write two different expressions to find the total cost for any number of people (n). What is the cost for 5 people? Prove that both of your expressions are correct.

· · · · Expression 1 ·

· · · · Expression 2 ·

2. How are your expressions the same? How are they different?

_____

_____

_____

_____

NAME: _____ **DATE:** _____

 Read and solve the problem.

Gavin's parents rent an arcade for his birthday party. The rental fee is $75.00. There is an additional $5.00 per person charge for game tokens and another $8.00 per person charge for snacks. Write an expression to find the total cost for any number (*n*) of people. What is the cost for 20 people?

1. Write an expression to represent the problem.

2. Evaluate the expression to find the cost for 20 people.

3. If the rental fee increases by $15, how does the expression change? Write and evaluate the new expression.

4. If Gavin invites 5 additional friends, how does the total cost change? Evaluate the new expression.

Think About It!

NAME: _____ **DATE:** _____

DIRECTIONS: Think about the problem, and answer the questions.

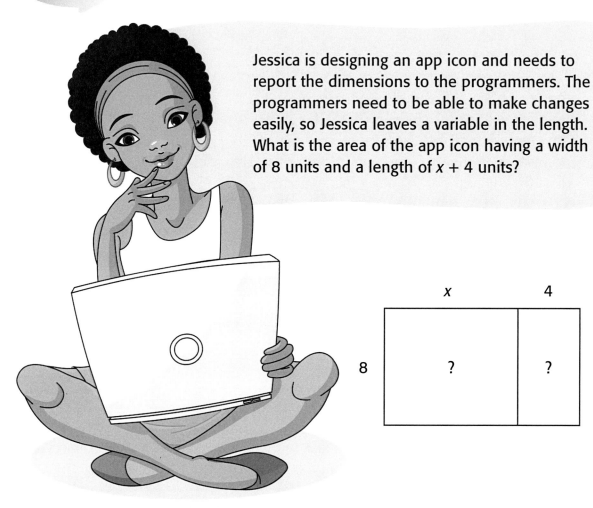

Jessica is designing an app icon and needs to report the dimensions to the programmers. The programmers need to be able to make changes easily, so Jessica leaves a variable in the length. What is the area of the app icon having a width of 8 units and a length of $x + 4$ units?

1. Will the expression for the area have a variable? Why or why not?

    _____

    _____

2. What operation can you use to find the area of the rectangle?

    _____

3. What constants are in the problem?

    _____

    _____

NAME: _____ **DATE:** _____

 **DIRECTIONS:** Read and solve the problem.

Problem: Jessica is designing an app icon and needs to report the dimensions to the programmers. The programmers need to be able to make changes easily, so Jessica leaves a variable in the length. What is the area of the app icon having a width of 8 units and a length of $x + 4$ units?

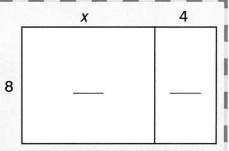

? **What Do You Know?**

🔑 **What Is Your Plan?**

💡 **Solve the Problem!**

🔍 **Look Back and Explain!**

Visualize It!

NAME: _____ DATE: _____

DIRECTIONS: Look at the example. Then, solve the problem by drawing a model.

Example: Draw a model to show an equivalent expression of $4(x + 5)$.

4x

20

$4(x + 5) =$ ___4___ groups of ___$x + 5$___

$4(x + 5) =$ ___$4x + 20$___

Draw a model to show an equivalent expression of $5(x + 3)$.

$5(x + 3) =$ _____ groups of _____

$5(x + 3) =$ _____

NAME: _____ **DATE:** _____

DIRECTIONS: Show two ways to solve the problem.

1. Stacy is going to a carnival and wants to play some games. The carnival charges a $12 entrance fee and $3 per game. How much money will Stacy spend if she plays 5 games at the carnival? Write two expressions that represent the problem. Then, use $n = 5$ to prove that your expressions are equivalent.

    Expression 1

    Expression 2

2. Which expression do you think is easier to solve? Explain your reasoning.

    _____

    _____

    _____

    _____

Challenge Yourself!

NAME: _____ **DATE:** _____

DIRECTIONS: Read and solve the problem.

Daniel's Delicatessen serves a lunch combination box consisting of a $6 sandwich, a $4 side salad, and a $2 drink. Daniel needs to enter an expression into his budget software to calculate the amount of money he makes, with n representing the number of lunch combination boxes sold. So far, he has written the following possibilities:

A. $2(3n + 2n + n)$

B. $6n + 4n + 2n$

C. $12n$

D. $2(5n + 1)$

E. $2(6n)$

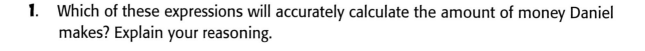

1. Which of these expressions will accurately calculate the amount of money Daniel makes? Explain your reasoning.

_____

_____

_____

2. Which of these expressions will **not** accurately calculate the amount of money Daniel makes? Explain your reasoning.

_____

_____

_____

3. Which expression do you recommend Daniel use? Explain your answer.

_____

_____

_____

NAME: _____ **DATE:** _____

 DIRECTIONS: Think about the problem, and answer the questions.

Clayton works at Load 'em Up Subs sandwich shop. A small sandwich (*s*) has 4 slices of cheese, and a large sandwich (*l*) has 8 slices of cheese. There are 100 total slices of cheese for the lunch shift. The inequality $4s + 8l \leq 100$ represents this situation. Which of the following sets of sandwiches could Clayton prepare without exceeding 100 slices of cheese?

A. 10 small sandwiches, 10 large sandwiches

B. 10 small sandwiches, 5 large sandwiches

C. 5 small sandwiches, 10 large sandwiches

D. 20 small sandwiches, 2 large sandwiches

E. 15 small sandwiches, 5 large sandwiches

1. If a sandwich order requires exactly 100 slices of cheese, will Clayton have enough cheese? How do you know?

_____

_____

2. What operation is used in the terms 4*s* and 8*l*? How do you know?

_____

_____

3. How is an inequality different from an equation?

_____

_____

_____

_____

Solve It!

NAME: _____ **DATE:** _____

**DIRECTIONS:** Read and solve the problem.

Problem: Clayton works at Load 'em Up Subs sandwich shop. A small sandwich (s) has 4 slices of cheese, and a large sandwich (l) has 8 slices of cheese. There are 100 total slices of cheese for the lunch shift. The inequality $4s + 8l \leq 100$ represents this situation. Which of the following sets of sandwiches could Clayton prepare without exceeding 100 slices of cheese?

A. 10 small sandwiches, 10 large sandwiches

B. 10 small sandwiches, 5 large sandwiches

C. 15 small sandwiches, 10 large sandwiches

D. 20 small sandwiches, 2 large sandwiches

E. 15 small sandwiches, 5 large sandwiches

? **What Do You Know?**

🔑 **What Is Your Plan?**

 Solve the Problem!

 Look Back and Explain!

NAME: _____ DATE: _____

 DIRECTIONS: Look at the example. Then, solve the problem by drawing a bar model.

Visualize It!

Example: Ramon is setting up the breakfast buffet at a hotel. Each morning, there are 144 tea bags available for the guests. This morning, there are 37 green tea bags in the serving case, and the rest are black tea bags. How many black tea bags (*b*) are in the serving case? Write and solve an equation. Check your solution using substitution.

144	
37	*b*

Check:

$37 + b = 144$

$b = 107$

$37 + 107 = 144$

$144 = 144$

Each morning, there are 96 packets of fruit preserve packets available for the guests. This morning, there are 29 grape preserve packets in the serving case, and the rest are strawberry preserve packets. How many strawberry preserve packets (*s*) are in the serving case? Write and solve an equation. Check your solution using substitution.

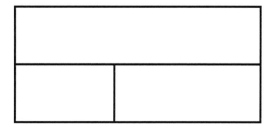

Check:

_____ _____

_____ _____

Solve It Two Ways!

NAME: _____ **DATE:** _____

Show two ways to solve the problem.

1. What inequality can represent this algebraic expression: 56 is greater than 7 times *n*? Write the inequality, and then find two numbers that will make the inequality a true statement. Prove your solutions using substitution.

········ **Solution 1** ···

········ **Solution 2** ···

2. Are there more solutions that will make this inequality true? Explain your reasoning.

    _____

    _____

    _____

    _____

NAME: _____ **DATE:** _____

DIRECTIONS: Read and solve the problem.

Nicole is packing for a trip. She has one very large suitcase for the jeans and shoes she hopes to take with her. The airline's rule states that her suitcase must weigh 50 pounds or less. Her jeans (j) each weigh 1 pound. Each pair of athletic shoes (a) weighs 2 pounds. Each pair of boots (b) weighs 4 pounds. Each pair of sandals (s) weighs 1.5 pounds. Her suitcase weighs 5 pounds when empty. The inequality $j + 2a + 4b + 1.5s + 5 \leq 50$ represents the situation. Which of the following sets of items can Nicole pack?

A. 10 jeans, 10 pairs of athletic shoes, 10 pairs of boots, 10 pairs of sandals

B. 5 jeans, 5 pairs of athletic shoes, 5 pairs of boots, 5 pairs of sandals

C. 8 jeans, 4 pairs of athletic shoes, 4 pairs of boots, 4 pairs of sandals

D. 2 jeans, 4 pairs of athletic shoes, 6 pairs of boots, 8 pairs of sandals

E. 6 jeans, 7 pairs of athletic shoes, 8 pairs of boots, 0 pairs of sandals

Show your work to prove your answers.

Think About It!

NAME: _____ **DATE:** _____

DIRECTIONS: Think about the problem, and answer the questions.

Toula is a hostess at Zorba's Greek Café. She gets paid $12 an hour, plus a $15 bonus per night for helping the food servers. Write an expression to represent Toula's pay, where *h* represents the number of hours she works.

1. What variable will be used in the expression? What does the variable represent?

_____

_____

_____

_____

2. What operations will be used in the expression? How do you know?

_____

_____

_____

_____

3. Will the expression include an equal sign? Why or why not?

_____

_____

_____

_____

NAME: _____ **DATE:** _____

 DIRECTIONS: Read and solve each problem.

Solve It!

Problem 1: Toula is a hostess at Zorba's Greek Café. She gets paid $12 an hour, plus a $15 bonus per night for helping the food servers. Write an expression to represent Toula's pay, where *h* represents the number of hours she works.

 **What Do You Know?**

 What Is Your Plan?

Solve the Problem!

 Look Back and Explain!

Problem 2: Sumate is a food server at Thai Cuisine. He gets paid $16 an hour and makes $50 in tips per night. He must pay the busboy who sets up and cleans his tables $20. Write an expression to represent Sumate's pay, where *h* represents the number of hours he works.

 **What Do You Know?**

 What Is Your Plan?

 Solve the Problem!

 Look Back and Explain!

Visualize It!

NAME: _____ DATE: _____

DIRECTIONS: Look at the example. Then, solve the problem by completing the table.

Example: Read the problem. Then, write a variable, a definition for the variable, and an expression that represents the problem.

At the entry gate, a county fair charges an $18 per person admission fee, plus a $10 parking fee for one vehicle. Write an expression that represents the total amount due per vehicle.

Variable	Definition of variable	Expression
p	number of people	18p + 10

Read the problem. Then, write a variable, a definition for the variable, and an expression that represents the problem.

The county fair charges $4 for a ride-all-day wristband, plus $0.75 each time the guest wants to jump to the front of the line. Write an expression that represents the amount due for a guest who wants to go on rides.

Variable	Definition of variable	Expression

NAME: _____ **DATE:** _____

DIRECTIONS: Show two ways to solve the problem.

1. Write two situations that can be represented by the expression $8n - 7$. Remember to define the variable in each situation.

Situation 1

_____
_____
_____
_____
_____
_____

Situation 2

_____
_____
_____
_____
_____
_____

2. How are the situations similar? How are they different?

_____
_____
_____
_____

NAME: _____ **DATE:** _____

DIRECTIONS: Read and solve the problem.

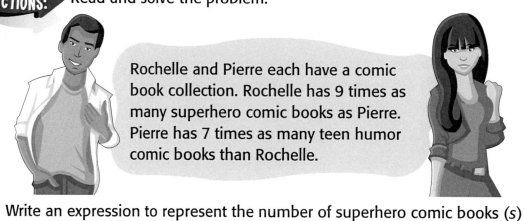

Rochelle and Pierre each have a comic book collection. Rochelle has 9 times as many superhero comic books as Pierre. Pierre has 7 times as many teen humor comic books than Rochelle.

1. Write an expression to represent the number of superhero comic books (*s*) Pierre has. Explain your reasoning.

   _____

   _____

   _____

2. Write an expression to represent the number of teen humor comic books (*t*) Rochelle has. Explain your reasoning.

   _____

   _____

   _____

3. If Rochelle has 72 superhero comic books, how many does Pierre have? Show your thinking.

4. If Pierre has 42 teen humor comic books, how many does Rochelle have? Show your thinking.

NAME: _____ DATE: _____

 DIRECTIONS: Think about the problem, and answer the questions.

Aimee buys some boxes of granola bars for a math club meeting. Each box costs $3.50. She spends a total of $21.00. Write and solve an equation to find how many boxes of granola bars she buys.

1. What variable will you use in your equation? What does the variable represent?

_____

_____

2. What operation will be used in the equation? How do you know?

_____

_____

3. Can Aimee buy at least 3 boxes of granola bars? How do you know?

_____

_____

4. Can Aimee buy at least 10 boxes of granola bars? How do you know?

_____

_____

Solve It!

NAME: _____ **DATE:** _____

DIRECTIONS: Read and solve each problem.

Problem 1: Aimee buys some boxes of granola bars for a math club meeting. Each box costs $3.50. She spends a total of $21.00. Write and solve an equation to find the number of boxes of granola bars she buys.

 What Do You Know?

 What Is Your Plan?

 Solve the Problem!

 Look Back and Explain!

Problem 2: Aimee has a budget of $395 to buy calculators for the math club. Each calculator costs $15.80. Write and solve an equation to find how many calculators Aimee can purchase if she uses the entire amount of money in her budget.

 What Do You Know?

 What Is Your Plan?

 Solve the Problem!

 Look Back and Explain!

© Shell Education

NAME: _____ **DATE:** _____

DIRECTIONS: Look at the example. Then, solve the problem by drawing a bar model.

Example: Pedro is saving money to purchase a $150 bicycle. So far, he has saved $85. Write and solve an equation to show how much money he still needs to save.

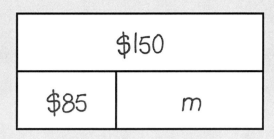

$$\$85 + m = \$150$$
$$m = \$150 - \$85$$
$$m = \$65$$

Pedro's uncle gives him a $50 gift card for a bike shop. Pedro uses it to buy a $22 helmet and a pair of gloves for $18.95. Write and solve an equation to show how much money Pedro has left on his gift card.

_____

_____

_____

Solve It Two Ways!

NAME: _____ DATE: _____

DIRECTIONS: Show two ways to solve the problem.

1. Calvin volunteers at a dog shelter. In one day, he gives out 72 dog treats. Each dog is given 4 treats. To how many dogs does Calvin give treats?

Strategy 1 ·

Write and solve an equation to solve the problem.

Strategy 2 ·

Use a different strategy to solve the problem.

2. What strategy do you think is more efficient? Explain your reasoning.

_____

_____

_____

_____

NAME: _____ DATE: _____

DIRECTIONS: Read and solve the problem.

Michael is filling his swimming pool. The pool holds 12,600 gallons of water. The hose pumps 360 gallons of water per hour. If the pool is empty when he starts, how many hours will it take to fill the pool?

1. Write an equation that will help you solve the problem. Define the variable in the equation.

   _____

   _____

2. Use the equation you wrote to solve the problem.

3. What operation did you use to solve the problem? Explain your strategy for finding the solution.

   _____

   _____

   _____

Think About It!

NAME: _____ DATE: _____

DIRECTIONS: Think about the problem, and answer the questions.

The number line represents the rental fee a community center charges for a party, based on the number of guests. Write an inequality to represent the amount of the rental fee (*r*) the community center charges.

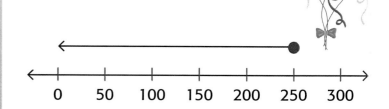

1. Is it possible for the rental fee to be $100? $200? $300? How do you know?

    _____

    _____

    _____

2. What is the maximum rental fee the community center charges? How do you know?

    _____

    _____

    _____

3. Would it make sense in this situation for the number line to include the numbers to the left of zero? Explain your reasoning.

    _____

    _____

    _____

NAME: _____ **DATE:** _____

DIRECTIONS: Read and solve each problem.

Problem 1: The number line represents the rental fee a community center charges for a party, based on the number of guests. Write an inequality to represent the amount of the rental fee (*r*) the community center charges.

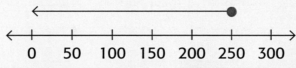

 What Do You Know?

 What Is Your Plan?

Solve the Problem!

Look Back and Explain!

Problem 2: The number line represents the fee the community center charges for a breakfast service for business meetings, based on the number of attendees. Write an inequality to represent the amount of the fee (*f*) the community center charges for the breakfast service.

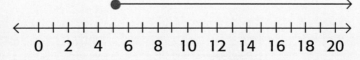

 What Do You Know?

What Is Your Plan?

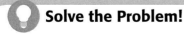 **Solve the Problem!**

 Look Back and Explain!

Visualize It!

NAME: _____   DATE: _____

DIRECTIONS: Look at the example. Then, solve the problem using a number line.

Example: Serena wants to display her soccer trophies on a shelf. After measuring the shelf's height, she realizes her trophies must be less than 10 inches tall to fit. Write an inequality to represent the height of the trophies, h, Serena can fit on the shelf. Represent the inequality on a number line.

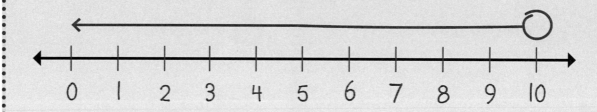

Inequality: _____ $h < 10$ _____

Serena's soccer coach tells her to practice her dribbling and passing skills for more than 15 minutes every day. Write an inequality to represent the number of minutes, m, Serena needs to practice. Represent the inequality on a number line.

Inequality: _____

NAME: _____ DATE: _____

 DIRECTIONS: Show two ways to solve the problem.

1. The manager of Fun Land Go-Karts is choosing between two safety advertisements about the speeds of the go-karts. The first advertisement says, "Go-karts can go up to 20 kilometers per hour." The second advertisement says, "Go-karts go less than 20 kilometers per hour." The manager says, "Isn't that two ways of saying the exact same thing?" Prove the manager wrong using an inequality and number line to represent each advertisement. Use *s* to represent the speed of the go-karts.

Advertisement 1

Inequality: _____

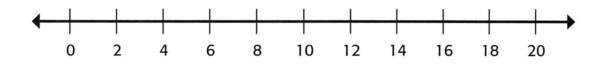

Advertisement 2

Inequality: _____

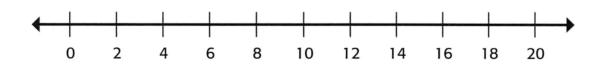

2. How are the inequalities similar? How are the inequalities different?

_____

_____

_____

_____

NAME: _____ **DATE:** _____

DIRECTIONS: Read and solve the problem.

While at Safari Adventure Park, Ella sees two signs. Sign 1 says, "Guests must be under 36 inches tall to enter Kiddie Town." Sign 2 says, "Guests must be 44 inches or taller to ride Turbo Roller Coaster." Represent each situation using an inequality and a number line. Use *h* to represent the height of the guests.

1. Write an inequality to represent the situation for Sign 1. Show the inequality on the number line.

Inequality: _____

← ————————————————————————————— →

2. Write an inequality to represent the situation for Sign 2. Show the inequality on the number line.

Inequality: _____

← ————————————————————————————— →

3. Give an example of a possible height of a guest who will not be permitted to enter Kiddie Town or ride Turbo Roller Coaster. Explain your answer.

_____

_____

_____

NAME: _____ DATE: _____

DIRECTIONS: Think about the problem, and answer the questions.

Nick works at a petting zoo. He makes sure there is enough hay for the sheep to eat. The graph shows the relationship between the number of sheep and pounds of hay. Write an equation that represents the relationship.

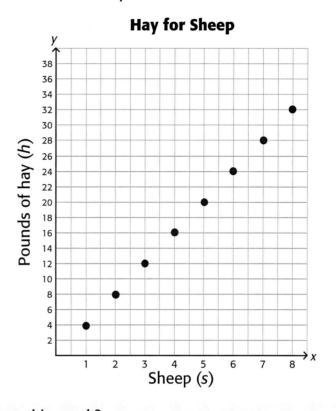

Hay for Sheep

1. Why are the points not connected on this graph?

   _____

   _____

2. What is the independent variable? How do you know?

   _____

   _____

3. What is the dependent variable? How do you know?

   _____

   _____

4. Complete the statement: As the number of sheep increases by _____ , the number of pounds of hay _____ (increases or decreases) by _____ pounds.

NAME: _____   DATE: _____

DIRECTIONS: Read and solve the problem.

Solve It!

Hay for Sheep

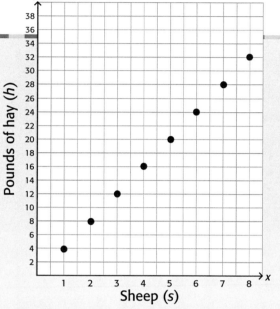

Problem: Nick works at a petting zoo. He makes sure there is enough hay for the sheep to eat. The graph shows the relationship between the number of sheep and pounds of hay. Write an equation that represents the relationship.

? What Do You Know?

🔑 What Is Your Plan?

 Solve the Problem!

 Look Back and Explain!

NAME: _____ DATE: _____

 DIRECTIONS: Look at the example. Then, solve the problem.

Example: Carmela wants to download 8 songs on her tablet. Each song costs $1.20. Complete the table and graph, and write an equation to show this relationship.

Songs (n)	Cost (c) (in dollars)
1	1.20
2	2.40
3	3.60
4	4.80
5	6.00
6	7.20
7	8.40
8	9.60

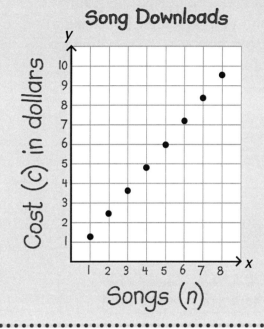

Song Downloads

Equation: _____ $c = 1.20n$ _____

Kendra wants to download 8 games on her computer. Each game costs for $2.00. Complete the table and graph, and write an equation to show the relationship.

Games (n)	Cost (c) (in dollars)
1	
2	
3	
4	
5	
6	
7	
8	

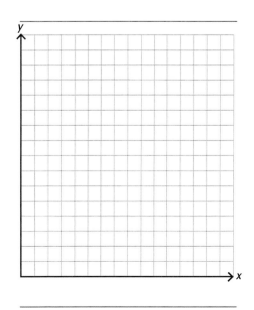

Equation: _____

Solve It Two Ways!

NAME: _____ DATE: _____

DIRECTIONS: Show two ways to solve the problem.

1. Levi is making bread pudding. The number of cups of raisins he uses determines the number of slices of bread he needs. The graph shows this relationship. Make a table, and write an equation to represent this relationship.

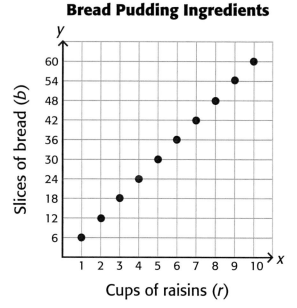

Bread Pudding Ingredients

Cups of raisins (r)

.... Representation 1 ....

Cups of raisins (r)	Slices of bread (b)
1	
2	
3	
4	
5	
6	
7	
8	
9	
10	

Representation 2

Equation: _____

Choose an ordered pair from the table to prove your equation is correct.

2. What are the advantages of representing a relationship using an equation?

_____

_____

_____

NAME: _____ DATE: _____

DIRECTIONS: Read and solve the problem.

Nadia and her mom are spending the day at Water World Regional Park. They want to rent a boat to sightsee along the lake. The table below shows the cost of renting a boat by the hour. What is the relationship between the two variables?

1. Complete the table and graph to represent the relationship.

Hours (n)	Cost (c) (in dollars)
1	
2	34
4	68
5	

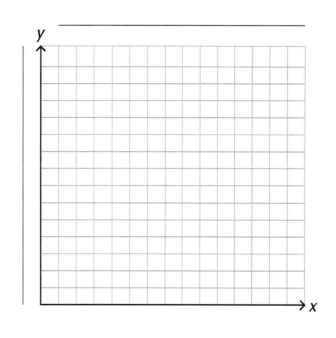

2. Write an equation to represent the relationship. Describe the relationship in words.

_____

_____

Think About It!

NAME: _____ **DATE:** _____

DIRECTIONS: Think about the problem, and answer the questions.

Lindsey is helping the school librarian resurface a tabletop with decorative self-adhesive paper. The tabletop is a trapezoid shape. How many square inches of paper are needed?

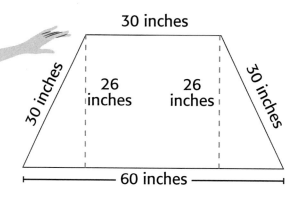

30 inches

30 inches

26 inches   26 inches

30 inches

60 inches

1. Lindsey thinks that if she multiplies the base of 60 inches by the height of 26 inches, she will get the area of the table's surface. Do you agree with her reasoning? Why or why not?

_____

_____

2. If the trapezoid is decomposed into a rectangle and two right triangles, what are the dimensions of the rectangle? What are the dimensions of the triangles?

_____

_____

3. How can decomposing the trapezoid into a rectangle and two triangles help with finding the area of the table's surface?

_____

_____

NAME: _____ **DATE:** _____

 **DIRECTIONS:** Read and solve the problem.

Problem: Lindsey is helping the school librarian resurface a tabletop with decorative self-adhesive paper. The tabletop is a trapezoid shape. How many square inches of paper are needed?

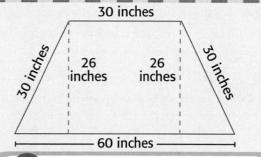

30 inches

30 inches   26 inches   26 inches   30 inches

60 inches

Solve It!

❓ What Do You Know?

🔑 What Is Your Plan?

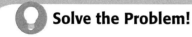 **Solve the Problem!**

 **Look Back and Explain!**

Visualize It!

NAME: _____ DATE: _____

DIRECTIONS: Look at the example. Then, solve the problem by drawing a picture.

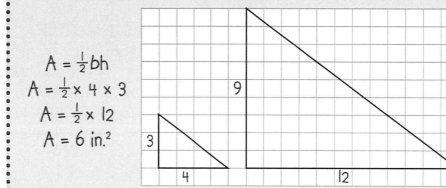

Example: A volleyball team is having its school logo printed on magnets. The prototype is a right triangle with a base of 4 inches and a height of 3 inches. The printing company says the dimensions will be tripled on the actual magnet. Draw a model of the prototype and actual magnet and compare their areas. Each unit square represents 1 square inch.

$A = \frac{1}{2}bh$
$A = \frac{1}{2} \times 4 \times 3$
$A = \frac{1}{2} \times 12$
$A = 6 \text{ in.}^2$

$A = \frac{1}{2}bh$
$A = \frac{1}{2} \times 12 \times 9$
$A = \frac{1}{2} \times 108$
$A = 54 \text{ in.}^2$

The area of the actual magnet is 9 times larger than the prototype because 6 × 9 = 54.

The track team is also having its school logo printed on magnets. The prototype is a right triangle, with a base of 2 inches and a height of 1 inch. The printing company says the dimensions will be quadrupled on the actual magnet. Draw a model of the prototype and actual magnet, and compare their areas. Each unit square represents 1 square inch.

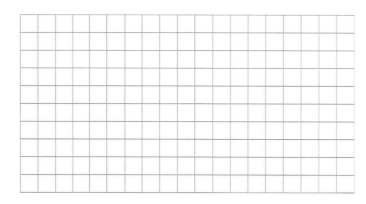

_____

_____

NAME: _____ **DATE:** _____

 DIRECTIONS: Show two ways to solve the problem.

1. Edgewood School is having large "E" logo signs printed on heavy poster board for fans to hold during sporting events. Find the total area of the poster board using two different strategies.

Strategy 1 · Strategy 2 · · · · · · · · · · · · · ·

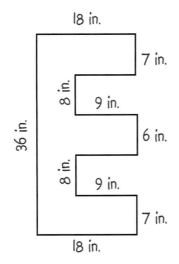

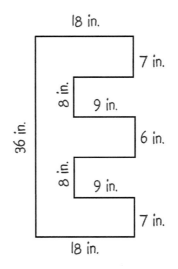

2. Which strategy do you think is more efficient? Explain your reasoning.

_____

_____

_____

Challenge Yourself!

NAME: ______________________ **DATE:** ______________

DIRECTIONS: Read and solve the problem.

Charity wants to make a rectangular quilt that measures 5 feet by 7 feet. She is making the quilt out of fabric pieces that are right triangles. Each fabric piece has a base of 4 inches and a height of 4 inches. How many fabric pieces will Charity need to make the quilt?

1. Sketch a drawing of one fabric piece and label the dimensions in inches. Then, find the area of the fabric pieces.

2. Draw the rectangular quilt and label the dimensions in inches. Then, find the area of the quilt.

3. Show how to find the solution to the problem. Explain your reasoning using words, numbers, or pictures.

NAME: _____ DATE: _____

 DIRECTIONS: Think about the problem, and answer the questions.

Natalie works at Tea Cup Café. On every table, there is a box of sugar cubes. Each box is a right rectangular prism with dimensions of 4 inches by 3 inches by 2 inches. Each sugar cube has side lengths of $\frac{1}{2}$ inch. Natalie needs to fill each box with sugar cubes without any gaps. How many sugar cubes can she pack into the box?

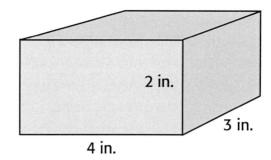

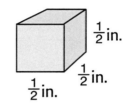

1. How many halves are in 4? How many halves are in 3?

_____

_____

_____

2. The height of the box is 2 inches. How many layers of sugar cubes with a height measuring $\frac{1}{2}$ inch will fit in the box? How do you know?

_____

_____

_____

3. Natalie thinks that if she multiples the length, width, and height of this box she will get the number of sugar cubes. Do you agree with her reasoning? Why or why not?

_____

_____

_____

NAME: _____ DATE: _____

 **DIRECTIONS:** Read and solve the problem.

Solve It!

Problem: Natalie works at Tea Cup Café. On every table, there is a box of sugar cubes. Each box is a right rectangular prism with dimensions of 4 inches by 3 inches by 2 inches. Each sugar cube has side lengths of $\frac{1}{2}$ inch. Natalie needs to fill each box with sugar cubes without any gaps. How many sugar cubes can she pack into the box?

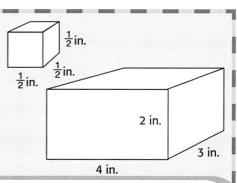

? What Do You Know?

🔑 What Is Your Plan?

 Solve the Problem!

 Look Back and Explain!

NAME: _____ DATE: _____

 DIRECTIONS: Look at the example. Then, solve the problem by labeling each dimension using the lengths given.

Example: How many ½-inch cubes are in the prism?

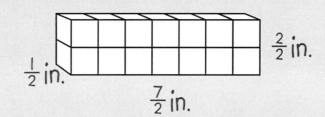

$\frac{2}{2}$ in., $\frac{7}{2}$ in., $\frac{1}{2}$ in.

There are 2 layers with 7 cubes in each layer. 14 cubes with dimensions $\frac{1}{2}$ in. × $\frac{1}{2}$ in. × $\frac{1}{2}$ in. make up the prism.

How many ¼-inch cubes are in the prism?

$\frac{3}{4}$ in., $\frac{7}{4}$ in., $\frac{5}{4}$ in.

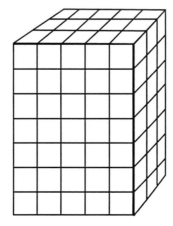

_____

_____

_____

Solve It Two Ways!

NAME: _____ DATE: _____

DIRECTIONS: Show two ways to solve the problem.

1. Two students describe the relationship between the large prism and the small prism on the right. Prove why each student is correct.

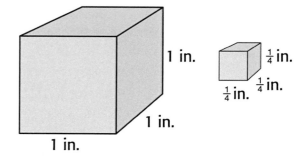

1 in.   1 in.   ¼ in.   ¼ in.   ¼ in.   1 in.

Student 1

It takes 64 of the ¼-inch small cubes to fill the large 1-inch cube.

Student 2

The small cube is $\frac{1}{64}$ of the large 1-inch cube.

2. How are the two answers similar? How are they different?

_____

_____

_____

_____

NAME: _____ DATE: _____

 Read and solve the problem.

Peggy's Perfect Pies sells mini fruit pies. Each mini pie is packaged in a cube-shaped box with side lengths of $\frac{1}{4}$ ft. The pie boxes are shipped to grocery stores in large shipping cartons with dimensions of $2\frac{1}{4}$ ft. × $1\frac{3}{4}$ ft. × 2 ft. How many mini pie boxes fit into a shipping carton?

1. Sketch the mini pie box. Label the dimensions and find the volume.

2. Sketch the large shipping carton. Label the dimensions and find the volume.

3. Show how to find the solution to the problem. Explain your reasoning using words, numbers, or pictures.

Think About It!

NAME: _____ **DATE:** _____

DIRECTIONS: Think about the problem, and answer the questions.

> Jamie's younger brother likes to play in the sandbox in their backyard. The sandbox is a rectangular prism. The area of the base is 12 square meters. The height of the sandbox is $1\frac{1}{3}$ meters. Jamie wants to know how much sand can fill the sandbox. What is the volume of the sandbox?

1. Why is the area of the base given in square meters, while the height is given in meters?

_____

_____

_____

2. What unit is used for the volume? How do you know?

_____

_____

_____

3. Jamie remembers that she can calculate the volume of a rectangular prism by using length × width × height. But, there are only two numbers given, 12 and $1\frac{1}{3}$. She doesn't think she has enough information to calculate the volume. What would you tell Jamie about her reasoning?

_____

_____

_____

NAME: _____ **DATE:** _____

 DIRECTIONS: Read and solve the problem.

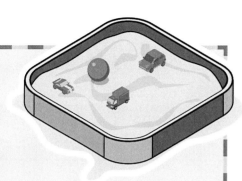

Problem: Jamie's younger brother likes to play in the sandbox in their backyard. The sandbox is a rectangular prism. The area of the base is 12 square meters. The height of the sandbox is $1\frac{1}{3}$ meters. Jamie wants to know how much sand can fill the sandbox. What is the volume of the sandbox?

 What Do You Know?

What Is Your Plan?

 Solve the Problem!

 Look Back and Explain!

Visualize It!

NAME: _____ **DATE:** _____

DIRECTIONS: Look at the example. Then, solve the problem by finding the missing dimension.

Example: Warm and Hearty Company ships cans of soup in large boxes. The boxes are rectangular prisms. The volume of the box is 160 cubic feet. If the length of the box is 8 feet, and the width is 5 feet, what is the height?

h = ?

L = 8 ft.   w = 5 ft.

$$160 = 8 \times 5 \times h$$
$$160 = 40 \times h$$
$$h = 4 \text{ ft.}$$

Warm and Hearty Company also ships canisters of oatmeal in large boxes. The boxes are rectangular prisms. The volume of the box is 81 cubic feet. If the length of the box is 4.5 feet, and the height is 6 feet, what is the width?

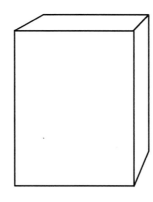

_____

_____

_____

NAME: _____ **DATE:** _____

DIRECTIONS: Show two ways to solve the problem.

1. Seth's mom is making her delicious tuna noodle casserole. The casserole pan has a length of $12\frac{3}{4}$ inches, a width of 8 inches, and a height of $3\frac{1}{2}$ inches. She fills the pan, but she leaves 1 inch of empty space at the top. What is the volume of the tuna noodle casserole?

Strategy 1

Strategy 2

2. Which strategy do you think is more efficient? Explain your reasoning.

_____

_____

_____

_____

Challenge Yourself!

NAME: _____ DATE: _____

DIRECTIONS: Read and solve the problem.

Hillary has a hamster named Hopscotch. She keeps Hopscotch in a cage at night. The cage is in the shape of a rectangular prism with a length of $30\frac{1}{2}$ inches, width of 18 inches, and height of $19\frac{3}{4}$ inches. The bottom 4 inches of the cage is covered with bedding material. Hillary wants to know how much space Hopscotch has in his cage. What is the volume of Hopscotch's cage, excluding the bedding?

1. What the volume of the entire cage? Show your thinking.

2. What is the volume of the bedding portion of the cage? Show your thinking.

3. Show how to find the solution to the problem. Explain your reasoning using words, numbers, or pictures.

NAME: _____ **DATE:** _____

DIRECTIONS: Think about the problem, and answer the questions.

Curtis works at a jewelry store. The boxes used to package the rings arrive at the store flat. Curtis needs to assemble the boxes by folding on the lines. He also needs to calculate the number of square centimeters of gift wrap needed to wrap the box. How many square centimeters of gift wrap will the box need?

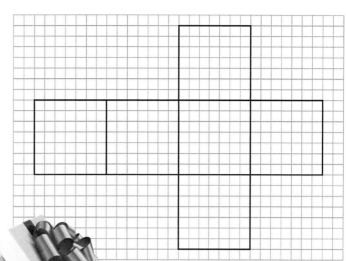

1. How many faces does the box have? _____

2. What shape is each face? How do you know?

_____

_____

3. What three-dimensional shape will the box form when it is assembled and folded? How do you know?

_____

_____

4. Curtis thinks that if he multiplies the length, width, and height for this box, he will need 343 square centimeters of gift wrap. Do you agree with his reasoning? Why or why not?

_____

_____

Solve It!

NAME: _____ **DATE:** _____

DIRECTIONS: Read and solve the problem.

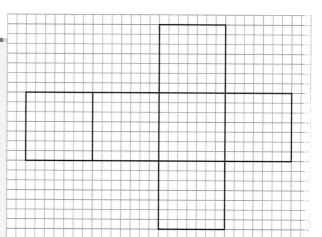

Problem: Curtis works at a jewelry store. The boxes used to package the rings arrive at the store flat. Curtis needs to assemble the boxes by folding on the lines. He also needs to calculate the number of square centimeters of gift wrap needed to wrap the box. How many square centimeters of gift wrap will the box need?

 What Do You Know?

What Is Your Plan?

 Solve the Problem!

 Look Back and Explain!

NAME: _____ DATE: _____

DIRECTIONS: Look at the example. Then, solve the problem.

Example: A baker receives an order to make a cake in the shape of a square pyramid. She wants to calculate the amount of cake she needs for all the faces. Draw a net of the shape and find the surface area.

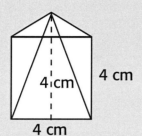

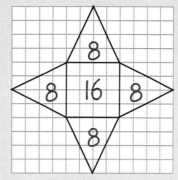

Area of square base = $4 \times 4 = 16 \text{ cm}^2$

Area of four triangular faces = $4 \times \left(\frac{1}{2} \times 4 \times 4\right) = 32 \text{ cm}^2$

Area of square pyramid = $16 + 32 = 48 \text{ cm}^2$

The baker also needs to make a mini cake in the shape of a square pyramid. She wants to calculate the amount of cake she needs for all the faces. Draw a net of the shape and find the surface area.

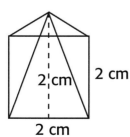

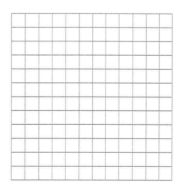

Area of square base = _____

Area of four triangular faces = _____

Area of square pyramid = _____

NAME: _____ **DATE:** _____

DIRECTIONS: Show two ways to solve the problem.

1. Maria is constructing a plastic enclosure for her gecko. The base is a square with 18-inch side lengths, and the faces are rectangles with dimensions of 18 inches by 24 inches. Sketch and label two possible nets Maria can use for the gecko enclosure. Find the surface area of each net.

Net 1 ·

Net 2 ·

2. How are the two nets similar? How are they different?

_____

_____

_____

_____

NAME: _____ **DATE:** _____

DIRECTIONS: Read and solve the problem.

Heather works at an upholstery shop. She is covering a bolster pillow with new fabric and wants to know how much fabric she will need.

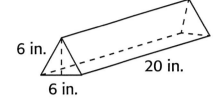

6 in.

6 in.

20 in.

1. Draw and label a net Heather can use for the pillow covering. Each unit on the graph paper represents 1 inch.

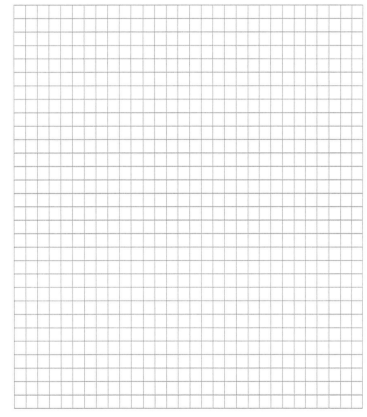

2. Calculate the surface area to find the number of square inches of fabric she will need.

Think About It!

NAME: _____ **DATE:** _____

DIRECTIONS: Think about the problem, and answer the questions.

The Oak Middle School newspaper staff is writing a story on the amount of homework students complete. Each reporter must submit a statistical question to the editor. Lucy submits, *Do you have homework tonight?* Walter submits, *What is the typical number of minutes students at Oak Middle School spend doing homework each night?* Which reporter submits a statistical question?

1. What are some possible responses to Lucy's question?

   _____

   _____

   _____

2. What are some possible responses to Walter's question?

   _____

   _____

   _____

3. How do you know if a question is statistical?

   _____

   _____

   _____

NAME: _____ **DATE:** _____

 DIRECTIONS: Read and solve the problem.

Solve It!

Problem: The Oak Middle School newspaper staff is writing a story on the amount of homework students complete. Each reporter must submit a statistical question to the editor. Lucy submits, *Do you have homework tonight?* Walter submits, *What is the typical number of minutes students at Oak Middle School spend doing homework each night?* Which reporter submits a statistical question?

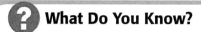 **What Do You Know?**

 What Is Your Plan?

 **Solve the Problem!**

 **Look Back and Explain!**

Visualize It!

NAME: _____ DATE: _____

DIRECTIONS: Look at the example. Then, solve the problem by completing the table.

Example: Write questions to show the difference between statistical and non-statistical questions.

Statistical question	Non-statistical question
How many times per week do students in my science class eat breakfast?	Do you eat breakfast?
What is the typical number of texts per day sent by students in my language arts class?	Do you text your friends?

1. Write questions to show the difference between statistical and non-statistical questions.

Statistical question	Non-statistical question
_____ _____ _____ _____	What is your favorite television show?
How many minutes per week do the members of the school basketball team practice outside of required practices?	_____ _____ _____ _____

2. What is the difference between statistical and non-statistical questions?

_____

_____

NAME: _____ **DATE:** _____

DIRECTIONS: Show two ways to solve the problem.

1. Mei is the president of the book club at Gardenview Middle School. She wants to conduct a survey among the members of the club. Write two examples of statistical questions she could write for the survey.

    Question 1

    _____

    _____

    _____

    _____

    _____

    _____

    Question 2

    _____

    _____

    _____

    _____

    _____

    _____

2. How are the statistical questions you wrote similar?

    _____

    _____

    _____

    _____

Challenge Yourself!

NAME: _____ DATE: _____

DIRECTIONS: Read and solve the problem.

The members of the computer club at Maple Middle School want to study the computer habits of all the students at the school. They ask the math club for help checking that the potential questions are indeed statistical questions. Here is the list of questions proposed by the computer club:

1. Do you have a computer?

2. Do you have Internet access at home?

3. What is your favorite app?

4. Do you use a computer to do school work?

5. Do you use a computer to play games?

As a member of the math club, how would you rewrite each question so that it is a statistical question?

1. _____

_____

2. _____

_____

3. _____

_____

4. _____

_____

5. _____

_____

NAME: _____ DATE: _____

 DIRECTIONS: Think about the problem, and answer the questions.

Trisha's Cafeteria Table

Trisha conducts a survey to find the number of days per week that students seated at her table in the cafeteria buy lunch. She records the results using a line plot.

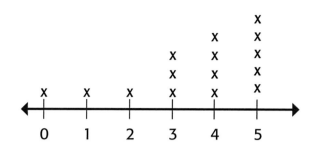

Times per week students buy lunch

1. What does each X on the line plot represent?

_____

_____

2. What does the X above 0 mean?

_____

_____

3. Why is the maximum number on the line plot 5?

_____

_____

4. Write a question that can be answered from the information on the line plot.

_____

_____

_____

Solve It!

NAME: _____ DATE: _____

 DIRECTIONS: Read and solve the problem.

Problem: Trisha conducts a survey to find the number of days per week the students seated at her table in the cafeteria buy lunch. She records the results using a line plot. Describe Trisha's findings, including the mean, median, and data distribution.

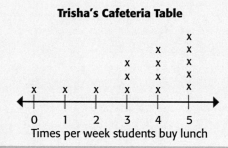

Trisha's Cafeteria Table

Times per week students buy lunch

 What Do You Know?

What Is Your Plan?

 Solve the Problem!

 Look Back and Explain!

NAME: _____ **DATE:** _____

 DIRECTIONS: Look at the example. Then, solve the problem by making a box plot.

Visualize It!

Example: In Alan's math class, students earn scores ranging from 0 to 5 on their homework. The data shows some scores from his class. Write the data from least to greatest, represent the data in a box plot, and describe the data distribution.

Homework scores:
5, 4, 2, 0, 3, 3, 5, 3, 2, 4, 4

Homework Scores from Alan's Math Class

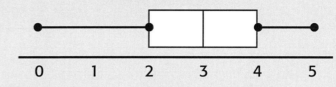

Score

Scores in order from least to greatest: 0, 2, 2, 3, 3, 3, 4, 4, 4, 5, 5

The minimum score is ____0____. The maximum score is ____5____. The median is ____3____. For the lower 50% of the scores, the median is ____2____. For the upper 50% of the scores, the median is ____4____.

In Emily's language arts class, students earn scores ranging from 0 to 4 on their written responses about independent reading books. The data shows some scores from her class. Write the data from least to greatest, represent the data in a box plot, and describe the data distribution.

Written response scores:
1, 2, 3, 2, 4, 3, 0, 3, 2

Written Response Scores from Emily's Language Arts Class

```
     0        1        2        3        4
                    Score
```

Scores in order from least to greatest: _____

The minimum score is _____. The maximum score is _____. The median is _____. For the lower 50% of the scores, the median is _____. For the upper 50% of the scores, the median is _____.

Solve It Two Ways!

NAME: _____ **DATE:** _____

DIRECTIONS: Show two ways to solve the problem.

1. The histogram shows the number of minutes band members at Parks Middle School practice their instruments each day, rounded to the nearest 5 minutes. Jane thinks that the typical number of minutes band members practice is 17.5. Elizabeth thinks that the typical number of minutes is 15. Their math teacher tells them they are both mathematically accurate. Explain which measure of center each student uses to describe the data.

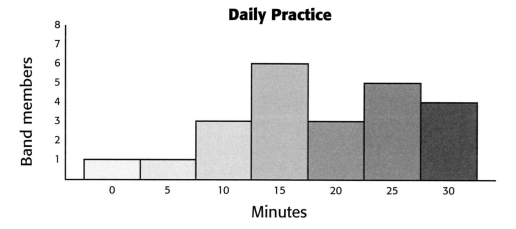

Daily Practice

Jane's Description	Elizabeth's Description
_____	_____
_____	_____
_____	_____
_____	_____
_____	_____

2. Which description do you think is a better representation of the data? Explain your reasoning.

_____

_____

_____

NAME: _____ **DATE:** _____

DIRECTIONS: Read and solve the problem.

A basketball championship game is coming up. The two competing teams are doing research on each other. The lists show the mean number of points per game scored by the players on the two teams over the entire regular season.

North Middle School Hawks: 9, 6, 13, 5, 9, 9, 6

South Middle School Eagles: 14, 21, 11, 5, 7, 8, 2

1. Make a line plot to represent North Middle School's data.

   Title: _____

   ← ── →

   _____

2. Make a line plot to represent South Middle School's data.

   Title: _____

   ← ── →

   _____

3. Compare the two competing teams' data distribution.

   _____

   _____

   _____

Think About It!

NAME: _____ **DATE:** _____

DIRECTIONS: Think about the problem, and answer the questions.

Fun and Fit Fitness Center tracks the number of minutes a sample of their members spends warming up before a workout. The findings are displayed on the histogram, with warm-up durations rounded to the nearest minute. In this sample, how do the times vary? What is the median and mean of the data?

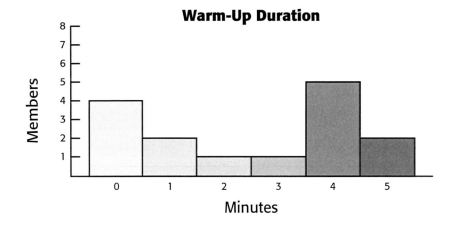

Warm-Up Duration

1. How many members are included in the sample? How do you know?

   _____

   _____

2. Why is 0 (zero) included on the histogram?

   _____

   _____

3. What is the math term for the "midpoint" of the data? How do you find the midpoint?

   _____

   _____

4. What is the math term for the "balancing point" of the data? How do you find the balancing point?

   _____

   _____

NAME: _____ **DATE:** _____

 DIRECTIONS: Read and solve the problem.

Problem: Fun and Fit Fitness Center tracks the number of minutes a sample of their members spends warming up before a workout. The findings are displayed on the histogram, with warm-up durations rounded to the nearest minute. In this sample, how do the times vary? What is the median and mean of the data?

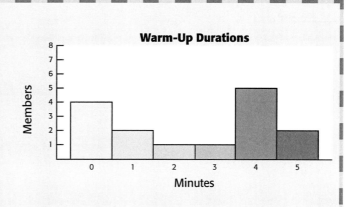

Warm-Up Durations

 What Do You Know?

 Solve the Problem!

What Is Your Plan?

 Look Back and Explain!

Visualize It!

NAME: _____ DATE: _____

Look at the example. Then, solve the problem by making a line plot.

Example: A librarian tracks the number of books students check out during one visit. Make a line plot to represent the data, and describe the center and variance.

Number of books checked out: 5, 6, 5, 7, 8, 7, 4, 3, 2, 1, 1, 1, 2, 2, 3, 4, 4, 3, 4, 2

Library Book Check Out

```
      x         x
 x    x    x    x
 x    x    x    x    x              x
 x    x    x    x    x    x    x    x
←──┼────┼────┼────┼────┼────┼────┼────┼──→
   1    2    3    4    5    6    7    8
              Books
```

least to greatest: ⓵ 1, 1, 2, 2, 2, 2, 3, 3, ③ ④
4, 4, 4, 5, 5, 6, 7, 7, ⑧

median
3 + 4 = 7
7 ÷ 2 = 3.5

range
8 − 1 = 7

Center: The median is ___3.5___ books. The mean is ___3.6___ books.

Variance: The range, or difference between the greatest number of books and least number of books checked out, is ___7___.

The librarian also tracks the number of DVDs checked out. Make a line plot to represent the data, and describe the center and variance.

Number of DVDs checked out: 5, 4, 3, 2, 2, 1, 3, 3, 2, 1, 5, 5, 4, 4, 4, 5, 4, 5, 5, 4

Title: _____

_____

Center: The median is _____ DVDs. The mean is _____ DVDs.

Variance: The range, or difference between the greatest number of books and least number of books checked out, is _____.

NAME: _____ **DATE:** _____

DIRECTIONS: Show two ways to solve the problem.

1. Melanie arrives late to math class. She misses the line plot the class made, showing the number of letters in the students' first names. She knows there are 18 students in the class, the range for the number of letters is 8, and the median of the letters is 5.

   Draw two line plots that match this information. Find the mean of the data for each of your line plots.

   Line Plot 1

   Title: _____

   Mean: _____

   ← ——————————————————————————— →

   _____

   Line Plot 2

   Title: _____

   Mean: _____

   ← ——————————————————————————— →

   _____

2. How are the two line plots similar? How are they different?

   _____

   _____

   _____

Challenge Yourself!

NAME: _____ **DATE:** _____

DIRECTIONS:
Read and solve the problem.

Jess manages a restaurant. She wants to review the restaurant's ratings on two popular mobile apps. So far, she has compiled these two line plots:

Reviews on "Yum Yum" App

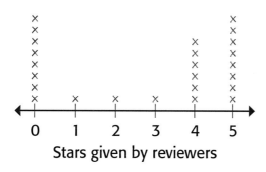

Stars given by reviewers

Reviews on "Suppertime Stars" App

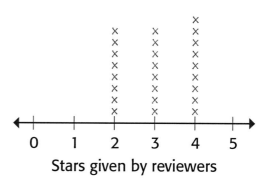

Stars given by reviewers

Using measures of center and variability, write a summary to compare the ratings Jess can submit to the owner of the restaurant.

_____

_____

_____

_____

_____

_____

NAME: _____ DATE: _____

 DIRECTIONS: Think about the problem, and answer the questions.

Trina trains Alaskan malamute dogs. She submits a summary of the weights of the dogs she is currently training to a kennel club. The veterinarian who visits Trina's dogs gives her a box plot that shows their weights. Help Trina write and explain a five-number summary of the data for the kennel club.

Weights of Trina's Alaskan Malamutes

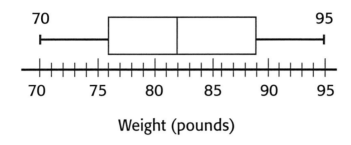

Weight (pounds)

1. What percentage of the data is included in the "box" of the box-and-whisker plot?

   _____

2. What percentage of the data is included in both "whiskers" of the box-and-whisker plot?

   _____

3. From this box plot, is there any way to determine exactly how many dogs Trina is currently raising and training? Why or why not?

   _____

   _____

   _____

4. Write a question that can be answered from the box plot.

   _____

   _____

   _____

Think About It!

NAME: _____ DATE: _____

DIRECTIONS: Read and solve the problem.

Problem: Trina trains Alaskan malamute dogs. She submits a summary of the weights of the dogs she is currently training to a kennel club. The veterinarian who visits Trina's dogs gives her a box plot that shows the dogs' weights. Help Trina write and explain a five-number summary of the data for the kennel club.

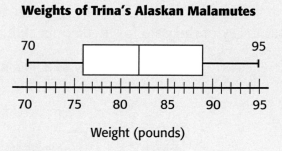

Weights of Trina's Alaskan Malamutes

70   95

70   75   80   85   90   95

Weight (pounds)

 What Do You Know?

What Is Your Plan?

 Solve the Problem!

 Look Back and Explain!

NAME: _____ DATE: _____

 DIRECTIONS: Look at the example. Then, solve the problem by making a histogram.

Visualize It!

Example: The Daytime Delights Café studies how much money each customer spends at breakfast. Make a histogram to represent the data in the frequency table.

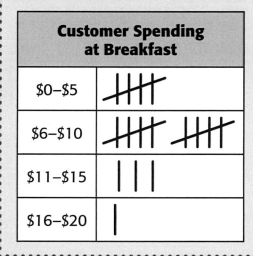

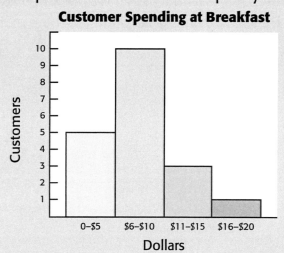

Daytime Delights Café decides to do a similar study during lunch service. Make a histogram to represent the data in the frequency table.

Customer Spending at Lunch	
$0–$5		
$6–$10	|||
$11–$15	HHHH HHHH
$16–$20	HHHH

_____
Title

NAME: _____ **DATE:** _____

Solve It Two Ways!

DIRECTIONS: Show two ways to solve the problem.

1. The owner of Sudsy Laundromat studies how many loads of laundry each customer washes. The data shown is a sample of 25 customers and the number of loads of laundry each washed. Represent this data using two different graphs. Be sure to write a title, and label the axis.

1, 1, 1, 1, 2, 2, 2, 2, 2, 2, 2, 3, 3, 3, 3, 3, 4, 4, 4, 4, 5, 5, 6, 7, 8

Graph 1

Graph 2

2. How did you decide which graphs are appropriate for the data in this situation? What information do your graphs show?

_____

_____

_____

NAME: _____ DATE: _____

DIRECTIONS: Read and solve the problem.

Amelia owns Creative Kids child care center. Several of the parents have asked her about the "typical" number of pieces in a puzzle that are appropriate for their child's age group. Amelia studies the number of pieces in the puzzles in two of the rooms of the child care center. She records her findings in these lists:

Puzzle pieces in 2- and 3-year-olds' room:
2, 6, 8, 10, 12, 12, 12, 12, 12, 12, 14, 16, 20, 24, 24

Puzzle pieces in 4- and 5-year-olds' room:
20, 20, 20, 22, 24, 24, 24, 24, 24, 36, 36, 36, 48, 48, 50

1. Make a box plot to represent the data for the 2- and 3-year-olds' room.

Title: _____

2. Make a box plot to represent the data for the 4-and 5-year-olds' room.

Title: _____

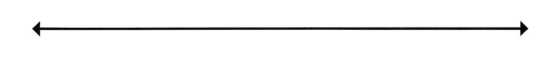

Think About It!

NAME: _____ DATE: _____

DIRECTIONS: Think about the problem, and answer the questions.

Festive Food Catering prepares large deli trays. It guarantees that its deli trays will include six different items, averaging 24 ounces each. However, the exact weight of each item will vary. The following is a list of items included on a tray and the weight of each. For this tray to satisfy the guarantee and have a mean of 24 ounces per item, how many ounces of Swiss cheese must be included?

Sandwich	turkey	ham	roast beef	provolone cheese	cheddar cheese	Swiss cheese
Cheese (ounces)	28	26	20	30	22	?

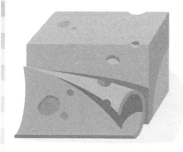   

1. What are you trying to determine in this problem?

_____

_____

2. What information do you already know?

_____

_____

3. How is this situation different from other problems you have encountered involving a mean?

_____

_____

NAME: _____ **DATE:** _____

 **DIRECTIONS:** Read and solve the problem.

Solve It!

Problem: Festive Food Catering prepares large deli trays. It guarantees that its deli trays will include six different items, averaging 24 ounces each. However, the exact weight of each item will vary. The following is a list of items included on a tray and the weight of each. For this tray to satisfy the guarantee and have a mean of 24 ounces per item, how many ounces of Swiss cheese must be included?

Sandwich	turkey	ham	roast beef	provolone cheese	cheddar cheese	Swiss cheese
Cheese (ounces)	28	26	20	30	22	?

 What Do You Know?

 What Is Your Plan?

Solve the Problem!

 Look Back and Explain!

Visualize It!

NAME: _____ DATE: _____

DIRECTIONS: Look at the example. Then, solve the problem by completing the table.

Example: A local grocery store has a salad bar, where customers are charged by the ounce. The store studies the mean weight of salads that customers make, and how the salads vary from this mean. Use the table to calculate the mean absolute deviation (MAD) of this sample.

Weight of salad (in ounces)	Distance of each weight from the mean (deviation)	Positive distance from the mean (absolute deviation)
18	$18 - 20 = -2$	2
24	$24 - 20 = 4$	4
16	$16 - 20 = -4$	4
30	$30 - 20 = 10$	10
12	$12 - 20 = -8$	8
Sum of the weights: 100		Sum of the absolute deviations: 28
Mean of the weights: $100 \div 5 = 20$		Mean absolute deviation: $28 \div 5 = 5.6$

The grocery store also has a hot-food bar, where customers are charged by the ounce. Use the table to calculate the mean absolute deviation (MAD) of this sample.

Weight of hot-food assortment (in ounces)	Distance of each weight from the mean (deviation)	Positive distance from the mean (absolute deviation)
34		
38		
42		
48		
16		
Sum of the weights: _____		Sum of the absolute deviations: _____
Mean of the weights: _____		Mean absolute deviation: _____

#51618—180 Days of Problem Solving

NAME: _____ **DATE:** _____

DIRECTIONS: Show two ways to solve the problem.

1. The editor of a school website asks each of her photographers to take about 12 pictures of the new aquarium during a field trip. The following is a list of the number of pictures each of the eight photographers submitted: 16, 10, 8, 14, 18, 12, 11, 7. Describe the variability of the data by finding the mean absolute deviation and range.

Strategy 1

Number of pictures taken	Distance from the mean (deviation)	Positive distance from the mean (absolute deviation)
16		
10		
8		
14		
18		
12		
11		
7		
Sum of the pictures: _____		Sum of the absolute deviations: _____
Mean of the pictures: _____		Mean absolute deviation: _____

Strategy 2

_____

_____

_____

_____

_____

_____

_____

_____

_____

_____

_____

2. Which of your strategies showing the variability do you think is more useful? Explain your reasoning.

_____

_____

_____

NAME: _____ DATE: _____

DIRECTIONS: Read and solve the problem.

"Sundae specialists" at Frozen Yogurt Fun Factory prepare cups of plain yogurt that weigh 8 ounces and cups of yogurt with toppings that weigh 14 ounces. The manager wants to study samples to see how accurate employees are at preparing individual cups. The following lists show the weights in ounces of the cups of yogurt:

Plain yogurt: 7, 6, 8, 10, 10, 12, 6, 9, 6, 6

Yogurt with toppings: 14, 15, 16, 10, 20, 11, 11, 18, 12, 13

Calculate the mean absolute deviation (MAD) of the plain yogurt weights and the topped yogurt weights.

Weight of plain yogurt (in ounces)	Distance of each weight from the mean (deviation)	Positive distance from the mean (absolute deviation)	Weight of yogurt with toppings (in ounces)	Distance of each weight from the mean (deviation)	Positive distance from the mean (absolute deviation)
Sum of the weights: _____		Sum of the absolute deviations: _____	Sum of the weights: _____		Sum of the absolute deviations: _____
Mean of the weights: _____		Mean absolute deviation: _____	Mean of the weights: _____		Mean absolute deviation: _____

ANSWER KEY

Week 1: Day 1 (page 13)

1. Gus needs to find 2 numbers less than 50 with a greatest common factor of 8. He cannot choose 8 as one of the solution numbers.

2. Find if Gus's solution pair 16 and 32 is correct.

3. Possible answer: Gus is not allowed to use 8 as a solution number because the other number would be any multiple of 8 and that would be too easy.

Week 1: Day 2 (page 14)

Gus's solution is not correct; Although 8 is a common factor of 16 and 32, it is not the greatest common factor; The greatest common factor of 16 and 32 is 16; find the greatest common factor of 16 and 32

Week 1: Day 3 (page 15)

The greatest common factor is 4; GCF = 2 × 2 × 5 = 20; Possible answer:

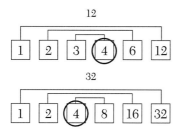

Week 1: Day 4 (page 16)

1. Possible answers: 32 and 48; 32 and 80; 48 and 64; 48 and 80; 64 and 80; Possible strategies: listing factors

2. Possible answer: I think listing the factors of both numbers is more efficient. I chose two even numbers that are greater than 16 but less than 90. I found the multiples of 16 and chose 32 and 48 as my solution.

Week 1: Day 5 (page 17)

1. There are 32 combination plates. Student may have listed the common factors or used the ladder method to find the greatest common factor of 96, 64, and 32, which is 32.

2. Each plate has 3 turkey club sandwiches, 2 ham and cheese sandwiches, and 1 meatball sandwich. Student may have divided each number by the greatest common factor, 32, to find how many of each sandwich will be on each plate.

Week 2: Day 1 (page 18)

1. There are 9 soups and 6 sandwiches that repeat in the same order and are served each day.

2. Find when tomato soup and grilled cheese sandwich will be served again.

3. Shelby is correct in that the combination will be repeated in 54 days. But, it might happen before that if there is a lesser common multiple.

Week 2: Day 2 (page 19)

18 days; find the least common multiple of 9 and 6

Week 2: Day 3 (page 20)

The least common multiple is 72; Multiples of 24: 24, 48, ⟨72⟩ 96, 120; Multiples of 36: 36, ⟨72⟩ 108, 144, 180

Week 2: Day 4 (page 21)

1. 20 days; Possible strategies: list common multiples or use the ladder method to find the least common multiple

2. Possible answer: I think listing the multiples is more efficient. I wrote the multiples of 4 and 10 until I found a multiple that both numbers have in common, which is 20.

Week 2: Day 5 (page 22)

1. Student may have listed the multiples or used the ladder method to find the least common multiple of 12, 4, and 5, which is 60.

2. Possible answer: The nurse restocked 60 of each item because the least common multiple of 12, 4, and 5 is 60. This means there were 5 packages of bandages, 15 packages of sanitizing wipes, and 12 packages of tongue depressors.

Week 3: Day 1 (page 23)

1. A shipment of 30 tomatoes and 18 avocados will be displayed in two rectangular arrays, using the greatest common factor as a common dimension.

2. The least common multiple of 18 and 30 is greater than the number of tomatoes and avocados.

3. Possible answer: I disagree with Ernesto because the greatest common factor of 18 and 30 is 6, not 3.

ANSWER KEY *(cont.)*

Week 3: Day 2 (page 24)

$30 + 18 = (6 \times 5) + (6 \times 3)$; $48 = 6(5 + 3)$; $48 = 6 \times 8$; $48 = 48$; dimensions: 6×5 and 6×3; use the greatest common factor to find the dimensions; use the distributive property to find the total number of items

Week 3: Day 3 (page 25)

$(9 \times 2) + (9 \times 9) = 9(2 + 9)$; $18 + 81 = 9 \times 11$; $99 = 99$; GCF of 18 and 81 = 9

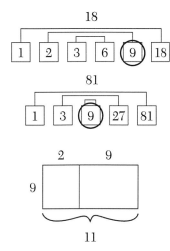

Week 3: Day 4 (page 26)

1. Possible expressions: $6(9 + 11)$ and $54 + 66$; all expressions simplify to 120 marchers

2. Possible answer: $(6 \times 9) + (6 \times 11)$ makes the dimensions of the rectangles clear. $54 + 66$ is a quick way to represent the situation and $6(9 + 11)$ is another way of showing $(6 \times 9) + (6 \times 11)$.

Week 3: Day 5 (page 27)

1. 72 vehicles; $8 \times 9 = 72$

2. The parking lot is organized into a 4×8 and 5×8 lot. This can be represented as $(8 \times 4) + (8 \times 5)$ and $8(4 + 5)$. When simplified, there are 72 parking spaces total with one lot holding 32 vehicles and the other holding 40 vehicles.

Week 4: Day 1 (page 28)

1. The r. 6 represents the remainder, or leftover amount, after dividing the dividend by the divisor. There are 6 leftover, which is not enough to make another group of 55.

2. The missing number has 4 digits. A quick estimate of 100×55 will result in a 4-digit number, so the exact answer must have 4 digits.

3. 143 and 55 can be multiplied as a first step in calculating the missing number.

Week 4: Day 2 (page 29)

7,871; multiply 143 and 55, add remainder 6

Week 4: Day 3 (page 30)

$\begin{array}{r} 1 \\ 42\overline{)538} \\ -420 \\ \hline 118 \end{array}$	There are 10 groups of 42 in 538. $10 \times 42 = 420$ $538 - 420 = 118$
$\begin{array}{r} 12 \\ 42\overline{)538} \\ -420 \\ \hline 118 \\ -84 \\ \hline 34 \end{array}$	There are 2 groups of 42 in 118. $2 \times 42 = 84$ $118 - 84 = 34$ The remainder is 34.

Week 4: Day 4 (page 31)

1. Possible solutions: 1,003, 1,008, 1,013, and 1,018. Any four-digit number with a 3 or 8 in the ones place will satisfy the constraints of the problem.

2. Possible answer: All answers must be 3 more than a multiple of 5. So, instead of having a 0 or 5 in the ones place like a multiple of 5 does, my numbers have a 3 or an 8 in the ones place to give a remainder of 3.

Week 4: Day 5 (page 32)

1. Kami's sister has 144 blocks. Since there are no blocks left when organized into 12 equal groups, the number must be a multiple of 12. The multiples of 12 between 100 and 150 are 108, 120, 132, 144. Only 144 will give a remainder of 4 when divided by 10 and a remainder of 1 when divided by 11.

2. Possible answer: The blocks can be arranged into 3 equal stacks because 3 is a factor of 144. There will be 48 blocks in each stack.

ANSWER KEY *(cont.)*

Week 5: Day 1 (page 33)

1. The question is asking, "How many $\frac{1}{16}$s are in $\frac{3}{4}$?" because one serving is $\frac{1}{16}$ of a pound. The question is asking how many of this size serving is in $\frac{3}{4}$ pound.

2. The solution must be greater than 1 because one serving is $\frac{1}{16}$, and $\frac{3}{4}$ is greater than $\frac{1}{16}$. So, there must be more than one $\frac{1}{16}$ in $\frac{3}{4}$.

Week 5: Day 2 (page 34)

12 servings of salsa; $\frac{3}{4} \div \frac{1}{16} = 12$; divide the amount of salsa by the amount per serving

Week 5: Day 3 (page 35)

3 rings

$1\frac{1}{4} = 1\frac{3}{12}$ $1\frac{1}{4} \div \frac{5}{12}$
$1\frac{1}{4} = 1\frac{3}{12}$ $1\frac{1}{4} \div \frac{5}{12}$

$\frac{5}{12}$ 1 ring $\frac{5}{12}$ 1 ring $\frac{5}{12}$ 1 ring

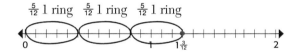

Week 5: Day 4 (page 36)

1. 15 pots of coffee; Possible strategies: number line; division; area model

2. Possible answer: I think a number line makes the situation easier to visualize. I partitioned a number line into six equal parts between the whole numbers. Since each pot requires $\frac{1}{6}$ pound, I circled groups of $\frac{1}{6}$ until I got to $2\frac{1}{2}$. There are 15 groups of $\frac{1}{6}$ in $2\frac{1}{2}$.

Week 5: Day 5 (page 37)

1. $\frac{3}{8} + 1\frac{1}{2} = 1\frac{7}{8}$ cups of chicken stock; $\frac{5}{8} + \frac{7}{8} = 1\frac{1}{2}$ teaspoons of cayenne pepper

2. $1\frac{7}{8} \div \frac{3}{8} = 5$, so there is enough stock for 5 pots of chili; $1\frac{1}{2} \div \frac{1}{4} = 6$, so there is enough cayenne pepper for 6 pots of chili; the amount of stock is lower, so Todd and Meredith have enough ingredients for 5 pots of chili

Week 6: Day 1 (page 38)

1. C

2. The solution must be greater than 2,000 meters. If 400 meters is used as an estimate for each of the 5 portions that would be 2,000 meters, and all of the portions of the path are greater than 400 meters.

Week 6: Day 2 (page 39)

Estimates should be between 2,000 and 2,009; exact answer is 2,009.10 meters; add the distances from start to finish

Week 6: Day 3 (page 40)

1. $72 \times 1.4 = 100.8$; $7.2 \times 1.4 = 10.08$; $10.08 \div 1.4 = 7.2$; $100.8 \div 1.4 = 72$

2. Possible answer: When the decimal point is one space to the left in one of the factors, the decimal point is one space to the left in the product. When the decimal point is one space to the left in both factors, the decimal point in two spaces to the left in the product. When I divide, I move the decimal point to the right and the decimal point in the quotient moves to the left.

Week 6: Day 4 (page 41)

1. Wendy and a friend will pay $179.50 more than her mom and a friend would have paid; Possible strategies: use equations to add the amounts together to find how much Wendy and a friend will pay ($95.00 + $95.00 = $190.00) and how much her mom and a friend would have paid ($5.25 + $5.25 = $10.50), and then subtract the amounts to find how much more it costs two people to go to the amusement park now ($190.00 − $10.50 = $179.50); use equations with multiplication (2 × $95.00 = $190.00 and (2 × $5.25) = $10.50, and then subtract ($190.00 − $10.50 = $179.50)

2. Possible answer: I think using equations with addition and subtraction is more efficient. It is easy to add and subtract money amounts because the decimals are two spaces to the left in all the numbers.

Week 6: Day 5 (page 42)

1. The lunch order will cost: $18.50 + 2($12.25) + $47.75 + $32.95 + $\frac{1}{2}$ ($37.80) = $142.60.

2. $200 − $142.60 = $57.40; $57.40 ÷ $8.20 is 7; The president of the parent organization has enough money to buy 7 pies. There is $57.40 left after buying everything on the lunch order list. I divided this amount by the cost of each pie.

ANSWER KEY *(cont.)*

Week 7: Day 1 (page 43)

1. For every 1 planet, there are 4 shooting stars.
2. Accurate, the problem gives this information; inaccurate, the pattern repeats, so there are more than 4 total stars on the whole sheet of wallpaper
3. Ratios can be written in word form (e.g., 3 to 4), using a colon (e.g., 3:4), or a fraction (e.g., $\frac{3}{4}$)

Week 7: Day 2 (page 44)

Possible ratios: 1 to 4 (or $\frac{1}{4}$ and 1:4) and 4 to 1 (or $\frac{4}{1}$ and 4:1); draw the pattern and write a ratio for the number of planets to stars and a ratio for the number of stars to planets; student should have drawn a planet surrounded by 4 stars

Week 7: Day 3 (page 45)

There are 108 total animals. There are 9 squares. $108 \div 9 = 12$; $4 \times 12 = 48$; $5 \times 12 = 60$; There are 48 cats and 60 dogs.

cats	12	12	12	12	
dogs	12	12	12	12	12

Week 7: Day 4 (page 46)

1. There are 30 onion bagels; $45 + 30 = 75$ total bagels; $45 \div 3 = 15$; $2 \times 15 = 30$; Possible strategies: equations; bar model
2. Possible answer: I think using equations is more efficient. I divided 45 plain bagels by 3 to get 15 and multiplied 15 by 2 to find the number of onion bagels. Then, I added 45 and 30 to find the total.

Week 7: Day 5 (page 47)

1. 16 ounces of pink lemonade concentrate
2. 32 ounces of club soda
3. 112 total ounces of punch; $64 + 16 + 32 = 112$; Possible answer: I found the total number of ounces by adding 64 ounces of cranberry juice, 16 ounces of pink lemonade concentrate, and 32 ounces of club soda.

Week 8: Day 1 (page 48)

1. Two pints of blueberries cost $5.00.
2. Find the unit rate and write it two ways.
3. A unit rate is a ratio of two measurements, with 1 as the second term.

Week 8: Day 2 (page 49)

1. $\frac{2}{5}$ (or 0.4) pint of blueberries per $1.00 and $2.50 per pint of blueberries; write the unit rate as a fraction; divide $5.00 by 2 to find the unit rate
2. $\frac{2}{3}$ (or 0.666…) of a grapefruit per $1.00 and $1.50 per grapefruit; write the unit rate as a fraction; divide 8 by $12.00 to find the unit rate

Week 8: Day 3 (page 50)

30 minutes

Minutes	1	2	4	5	10	15	30
Strides	130	260	520	650	1,300	1,950	3,900

Week 8: Day 4 (page 51)

1. Boots runs at the fastest rate (30 miles per 60 minutes); Possible strategies: convert the ratios to show how many miles each racehorse can run in 60 minutes; make a rate table with the number of miles and minutes
2. Possible answer: I think converting the ratios to show how many miles each racehorse can run in 60 minutes (or 1 hour) is more efficient. This helped me compare the rates of each racehorse more easily.

Week 8: Day 5 (page 52)

1. 32 minutes; $1.00 \div $0.25 = 4$; $4 \times 8 = 32$
2. 40 minutes; $1.00 \div $0.10 = 10$; $10 \times 4 = 40$
3. 20 minutes; $1.00 \div $0.50 = 2$; $2 \times 10 = 20$
4. Fresh 'n' Dry Laundromat is offering the best deal. It charges $1.00 for 40 minutes. Sudsy Laundromat charges $1.00 for 32 minutes and Squeaky Clean Laundromat charges $1.00 for 20 minutes.

Week 9: Day 1 (page 53)

1. One hundred Fresh Food points are worth $4.00 in "bonus bucks."
2. How many points are $16.00 in "bonus bucks" worth?
3. Each point is worth less than $1.00 because 100 points are only worth $4.00, not $100.00.

Week 9: Day 2 (page 54)

400 points; $4.00 \div $1.00 = 4$; $100 \div 4 = 25$; $16 \times 25 = 400$; divide to find how many points it takes to earn $1.00 in "bonus bucks"; multiply to find how many points a customer uses with $16.00 in "bonus bucks"

ANSWER KEY *(cont.)*

Week 9: Day 3 (page 55)

4 bottles of soap cost $16.00 and $40.00 will buy 10 bottles of soap.

Bottles of soap	Cost (in dollars)
1	4
2	8
3	12
4	16
5	20
6	24
7	28
8	32
9	36
10	40

Soap Bottle Cost

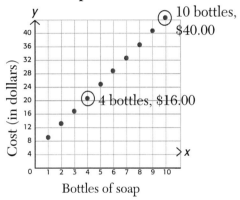

Bottles of soap

Week 9: Day 4 (page 56)

1. 24 scoops of dry kibble; $16 \div 2 = 8$; $3 \times 8 = 24$; Possible strategies: rate table; graph; equations

2. Possible answer: I think using equations is more efficient because I can divide 16 by 2 to find how many scoops of dry food. Then, I can use multiplication to find the solution, $3 \times 8 = 24$.

Week 9: Day 5 (page 57)

1. Jeans Junction has the lowest price. Pants Palace has the highest price. Pants Palace: 1 pair of jeans costs $20 ($40 \div 2 = $20); Denim Spot: 1 pair of jeans costs $18 ($54 \div 3 = $18); Jeans Junction: 1 pair of jeans costs $15 ($30 \div 2 = $15)

2. Jeans Junction is offering the lowest cost ($15.00 per pair of jeans). Possible answer: I found the unit rate for the cost of 1 pair of jeans at each store by dividing the cost by the number of jeans.

Week 10: Day 1 (page 58)

1. Four croissants cost $5.00.

2. Find how much nine croissants will cost.

3. Each croissant costs more than $1.00 because 4 croissants cost more than $4.00, which is what the cost would be if they only cost $1.00 each.

4. The solution will be more than $10.00 because $10.00 buys 8 croissants, and the problem is asking for the cost of 9 croissants.

Week 10: Day 2 (page 59)

1. $11.25; $5.00 \div 4 = $1.25; $1.25 \times 9 = $11.25; find the unit rate by dividing $5.00 by 4 and then multiply the unit rate by 9 to find how much the croissants will cost

2. 20 minutes; $55 \div 5 = 11$; $220 \div 11 = 20$; find the unit rate by dividing 55 by 5 and then divide the 220 by the unit rate to find how many minutes she needs to walk

Week 10: Day 3 (page 60)

Gabe can purchase 4 food tickets for $1.00.

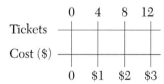

Week 10: Day 4 (page 61)

1. 80 inches; $24 \div 3 = 8$; $10 \times 8 = 80$; Possible strategies: double number line; equations

2. Possible answer: I think using a double number line is better because it helps me see the relationship between the number of inches and seconds.

Week 10: Day 5 (page 62)

1. 9 meters per second; $90 \div 10 = 9$

2. 10 meters per second; $110 \div 11 = 10$

3. Possible explanation: To find the unit rate, I divided the number of meters by the number of seconds. Charlotte is running at a rate of 10 meters per second ($110 \div 11 = 10$), and Charlie is running at a rate of 9 meters per second ($90 \div 10 = 9$), which means the cheetahs are not running at the same speed.

ANSWER KEY *(cont.)*

Week 11: Day 1 (page 63)

1. Connor answers 17 questions correctly out of 20 on his math quiz.
2. Connor is using a 100 because percent means out of 100, and the teacher records grades in percentages.
3. Connor is figuring out how many out of 100 is equivalent to 17 out of 20.

Week 11: Day 2 (page 64)

1. $\frac{17}{20} = 85\%$; $20 \times 5 = 100$; $17 \times 5 = 85$; $\frac{85}{100} = 85\%$; write an equivalent ratio for $\frac{17}{20}$ with 100 as the denominator
2. $\frac{17}{25} = 68\%$; $25 \times 4 = 100$; $17 \times 4 = 68$; $\frac{68}{100} = 68\%$; write an equivalent ratio for $\frac{17}{25}$ with 100 as the denominator; This percentage is different than the percentage in question 1 because even though Connor still answered 17 questions correctly, there were 25 questions instead of 20.

Week 11: Day 3 (page 65)

78 + 78 + 78 + 26 = 260; There are 260 seventh graders at Muir Academy.

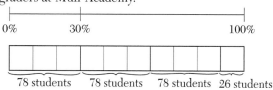

Week 11: Day 4 (page 66)

1. 9 cookies need to be decorated with buttercream frosting

   Carla's Strategy:

75	3	9
100	4	12

   Wes's Strategy:

   $\frac{75}{100} \times 12 = \frac{900}{100} = 9$ cookies

2. Possible answer: I prefer Carla's strategy. She used a rate table. She wrote 75% as a ratio of 75 out of 100. I completed her strategy by writing the equivalent ratios. I found 3 out of 4 by writing $\frac{75}{100}$ in simplest form. Then, I multiplied both 3 and 4 by 3 to get 9 out of 12.

Week 11: Day 5 (page 67)

1. An 18% tip on $55.00 is $9.90, so $55.00 + $9.90 is $64.90 total for dinner.
2. Sales tax of 8% on $60.00 is $4.80, so $60.00 + $4.80 is $64.80 total for the sneakers.
3. The total cost is $64.90 + $64.80 = $129.70. Student should have found the cost of dinner, including tax, the cost of the sneakers, including tax, and found the total cost by adding the amounts together.

Week 12: Day 1 (page 68)

1. The door is 12 inches wide and 60 inches tall.
2. Nicole's reasoning is incorrect. The area of the paper is given in square inches, and she found her locker door's area in square feet. She needs to convert the door measurements to inches and then find the area.

Week 12: Day 2 (page 69)

Nicole will have 0 square inches of paper left. The 1-foot by 5-foot door is equal to 12 inches by 60 inches. The area of the door is $12 \times 60 = 720$ square inches. Since there are 720 square inches of paper, Nicole will not have any paper left over.

Week 12: Day 3 (page 70)

25 kilograms is about 55 pounds. The bulldog weighs less than David's golden retriever, which weighs 65 pounds.

Pounds (lb.)	2.2	22	55
Kilograms (kg)	1	20	25

ANSWER KEY *(cont.)*

Week 12: Day 4 (page 71)

1. Square feet: 70 yards by 70 yards is converted to 210 feet by 210 feet (1 yd. = 3 ft.; 70 × 3 = 210); The area of the park is 44,100 square feet (210 × 210 = 44,100); 90 feet by 90 feet results in a playground area of 8,100 square feet (90 × 90 = 8,100); 44,100 – 8,100 = 36,000 square feet of land not covered by the playground; Square yards: 90 feet by 90 feet is converted to 30 yards by 30 yards (90 ÷ 3 = 30); The area of the playground is 900 square yards (30 × 30 = 900); 70 yards by 70 yards results in a park area of 4,900 square yards (70 × 70 = 4,900); 4,900 – 900 = 4,000 square yards of land not covered by the playground

2. Possible answer: For both solutions, I had to calculate the area of the park and the playground, then subtract the playground's area from the park's area. In one solution I had to convert yards to feet by multiplying by 3, and in the other solution I had to convert feet to yards by dividing by 3 (or multiplying by $\frac{1}{3}$).

Week 12: Day 5 (page 72)

Email needs to include the following details: 847 pounds is about 385 kilograms (847 ÷ 2.2 = 385), and 60 inches is about 152.4 centimeters (60 × 2.54 = 152.4)

Week 13: Day 1 (page 73)

1. withdrawal
2. donation
3. Possible answer: A positive number is used to represent an amount of money that you have. A negative number is used to show what you owe.

Week 13: Day 2 (page 74)

1. withdrawal: –30; donation: +50; find clue words to write each transaction as a positive or negative number
2. expenditure: –25; charge: –175; income: +500; find clue words to write each transaction as a positive or negative number

Week 13: Day 3 (page 75)

33 + 223 + 455 = 711 ft.

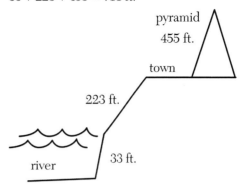

Week 13: Day 4 (page 76)

1. Overall gain of 11 yards; Possible strategies: number line, diagram, add or subtract positive and negative numbers
2. Possible answer: I prefer drawing a diagram. I drew a football field by sketching and labeling the positive and negative yardage. I combined all of the gains, then all of the losses, and found the overall yardage.

Week 13: Day 5 (page 77)

The order of the teams is South (90), East (50), West (30), and North (10).

Week 14: Day 1 (page 78)

1. below ground level
2. –2
3. Ground level represents zero because levels 1–3 are positive numbers, and the basement levels are negative numbers.

Week 14: Day 2 (page 79)

5 levels; Eva is 2 levels below the ground level and Gabby is 3 levels above ground level; 2 + 3 = 5; draw a diagram to count how many levels are between Basement Level 2 and Level 3

ANSWER KEY (cont.)

Week 14: Day 3 (page 80)

1.

Number	Opposite
$\frac{9}{2}$	$-\frac{9}{12}$
–2.5	2.5
3	–3
$-1\frac{1}{3}$	$1\frac{1}{3}$

2. The distance from zero for each number and its opposite is exactly the same.

Week 14: Day 4 (page 81)

1. Kenny is correct. The opposite of –4 is 4, and –(–4) is also 4.

2. Possible answer: The number lines are exactly the same because the opposite of –4 can also be represented as –(–4).

Week 14: Day 5 (page 82)

1.

2. Boxes with results of –5, +6, and –6 need to be sent back for repackaging because they are more than 4 raisins away from the goal. –5 is 1 raisin away, +6 is 2 raisins away, and –6 is 2 raisins away from the goal.

Week 15: Day 1 (page 83)

1. entry plaza

2. Reflections means each point is an equal distance across the opposite side of a given line or axis.

3. Quadrant I

4. Andy is not correct. He is reflecting the point across the y-axis. If reflected across the x-axis, the point will be in Quadrant IV.

Week 15: Day 2 (page 84)

1. The koala bear exhibit is at (5, –6); find the coordinates of the panda exhibit and reflect the point over the x-axis

2. The grizzly bear exhibit is at (–5, –6); find the coordinates of the koala exhibit and reflect the point over the y-axis

Week 15: Day 3 (page 85)

1.

Point	Coordinates
Point B	(–3, –1)
Point B reflected across the x-axis	(–3, 1)
Point B reflected across the y-axis	(3, –1)

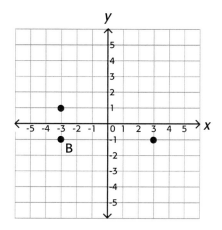

2. Possible answer: In reflections across the x-axis, the x-coordinate stays the same, and the y-coordinate is the opposite. In reflections across the y-axis, the x-coordinate is the opposite, and the y-coordinate stays the same.

Week 15: Day 4 (page 86)

1. Peter's Strategy:

x	y
2	1
3	–4
–1	3
–5	–2

Sophia's Strategy: (2, 1), (3, –4), (–1, 3), and (–5, –2)

2. Possible answer: I think writing the x- and y-coordinates in a table is better because it helps me know which coordinate is x and which is y.

ANSWER KEY *(cont.)*

Week 15: Day 5 (page 87)

Possible answer:

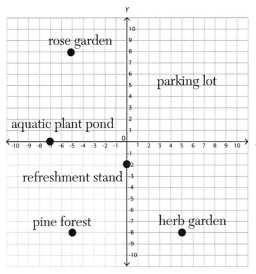

Exhibit	Coordinates
rose garden	(–5, 8); or any point (–, +)
pine forest	(–5, –8); (same *x* as rose garden point, opposite *y* as rose garden point)
herb garden	(5, –8); (opposite *x* as pine forest point, same *y* as pine forest point)
aquatic plant pond	(–7, 0); or any point (–, 0)
refreshment stand	(0, –2); or any point (0, –)
parking lot	quadrant 1

Week 16: Day 1 (page 88)

1. Theo is incorrect. Books and DVDs have different fees, and Theo and Joy have different amounts of each that are overdue.

2. No, neither Theo nor Joy owes more than $1.00 because they both have 6 days worth of overdue items. Not all of the items are games or DVDs, so the fee will be less than $1.00.

3. The library might keep track of fees in negative amounts because it is money they are owed. Borrower accounts should have a zero balance if no money is owed, and a negative amount shows any money due on the account.

Week 16: Day 2 (page 89)

–$0.80 < –$0.70; Theo owes more than Joy because Theo owes $0.80 and Joy owes $0.70; Theo: $(4 \times -\$0.10) + (2 \times -\$0.20) = -\$0.80$; Joy: $(5 \times -\$0.10) + (1 \times -\$0.20) = -\$0.70$

Week 16: Day 3 (page 90)

1. –3 > –6; The low temperature in Lewistown, Montana, was colder than Billings, Montana, by 3°C.

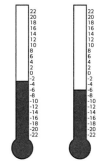

Billings   Lewistown

Week 16: Day 4 (page 91)

1. Set 1: $\frac{1}{2} > \frac{3}{8}$; Set 2: $-\frac{3}{4} > -\frac{15}{16}$

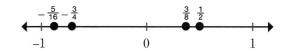

2. Possible answer: A number line helps me to compare numbers because it shows the distance each number is from zero.

ANSWER KEY *(cont.)*

Week 16: Day 5 (page 92)

1. −13, −11, −9, −7, −6, −5, −3, −2, −1, 0, 1, 2, 3, 5
2.

3. There were 4 days above 0 and 9 days below 0. Students may have used their ordered list or their number line, or may have grouped the negative numbers and grouped the positive integers.

Week 17: Day 1 (page 93)

1. The temperature in Fargo was −2° F. The temperature in Cheyenne was 1° F.
2. Absolute value means the distance the number is from 0.
3. Stephen's absolute value inequality is incorrect. The absolute value of −2 is 2, but the absolute value of 1 is not −1. Stephen might have been thinking of the opposites of the temperatures instead of the absolute value (distance from zero).

Week 17: Day 2 (page 94)

1. −2 < 1; |−2| > |1|; |−2| = 2; |1| = 1; write an inequality to compare the temperatures; write an inequality to compare the absolute values of the temperatures
2. −9 < −7; |−9| > |−7|; |−9| = 9; |−7| = 7; write an inequality to compare the temperatures; write an inequality to compare the absolute values of the temperatures

Week 17: Day 3 (page 95)

The frog may have landed on −7 or 7. Both −7 and 7 are 7 spaces from 0 on the number line. |−7| and |7| is 7.

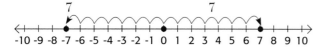

Week 17: Day 4 (page 96)

1. The closest score to the time allotment is −0:45. The farthest score from the time allotment is −1:45. The number with the least absolute value is −0:45. The number with the greatest absolute value is −1:45.
2. Possible answer: The number with the greatest absolute value is the number with the greatest distance (farthest) from the time allotment, and the number with the least absolute value is the number with the least distance (closest) to the time allotment.

Week 17: Day 5 (page 97)

1.

Animal	Distance from sea level	Absolute value notation	Absolute value
hammerhead shark	260 ft. below sea level	|−260|	260
California condor	15,000 ft. above sea level	|15,000|	15,000
anglerfish	3,000 ft. below sea level	|−3,000|	3,000
pelican	9,000 ft. above sea level	|9,000|	9,000
emperor penguin	900 ft. below sea level	|−900|	900
Mexican free-tailed bat	600 ft. above sea level	|600|	600
dolphin	290 ft. below sea level	|−290|	290
peregrine falcon	3,000 ft. above sea level	|3,000|	3,000

2. California condor, pelican, anglerfish and peregrine falcon (tied), emperor penguin; Mexican free-tailed bat; dolphin; hammerhead shark

Week 18: Day 1 (page 98)

1. To find the location of the cereal, start at the origin, move right along the x-axis, and then move down along the y-axis.
2. To find the location of the milk, start at the origin, move right along the x-axis, and then move up along the y-axis.
3. The points create a vertical line. The x-coordinate for all of the points is 8.

ANSWER KEY *(cont.)*

Week 18: Day 2 (page 99)

1. 11 yards; 5 + 6 = 11; the cereal is located at
    –5 along the *y*-axis, which is 5 units away from
    zero, and the milk is located at 6 along the
    y-axis, which is 6 units away from zero

2. 8 yards; 6 + 2 = 8; the peanut butter is located
    at –6 along the *x*-axis, which is 6 units away
    from zero, and the jelly is located at 2 along the
    x-axis, which is 2 units away from zero

Week 18: Day 3 (page 100)

The distance between Prize C and Prize D is
8 units.

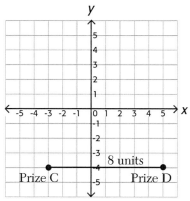

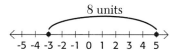

Week 18: Day 4 (page 101)

1. The roller coasters have a distance of $15\frac{3}{4}$ units.
    Student should have plotted a point for the
    Rocket at $(8\frac{1}{2}, -2)$ and for Kiddie Minicoaster
    at $(-7\frac{1}{4}, -2)$: Possible strategies: count the
    number of units along the *x*-axis on the
    coordinate plane from $8\frac{1}{2}$ to $-7\frac{1}{4}$; use a number
    line to count the number of spaces from $8\frac{1}{2}$
    to $-7\frac{1}{4}$; add $8\frac{1}{2}$ units and $7\frac{1}{4}$ units, which is
    $15\frac{3}{4}$ units

2. Possible answer: I think using the coordinate
    plane is more efficient because I can count the
    units along the *x*-axis since the *y*-coordinates
    are the same.

Week 18: Day 5 (page 102)

1. Western Ride: 30 ft.; Dragon: 50 ft.; Kiddie
    Mini: 20 ft.; Tree Topper: 100 ft.; Flyer: 90 ft.;
    Rocket: 80 ft.; Wild Ride: 130 ft.; Racer: 80 ft.

2. Wild Ride, Tree Topper, Flyer, Rocket
    and Racer (tied), Dragon, Western Ride,
    Kiddie Mini

Week 19: Day 1 (page 103)

1. 6 points; There are 6 ordered pairs. Each
    coordinate pair is one point when plotted on
    the coordinate plane.

2. The number of points indicate the shape
    should have 6 sides and 6 vertices.

3. Maya probably does this to be sure the designs
    are correct and look appealing before putting
    them on a T-shirt, so she does not waste a
    T-shirt with a bad design.

Week 19: Day 2 (page 104)

1. Hexagon; plot the points and connect them to
    find the shape

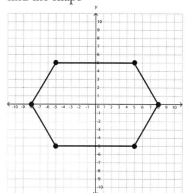

2. Pentagon; plot the points and connect them to
    find the shape

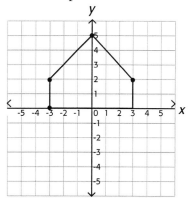

ANSWER KEY *(cont.)*

Week 19: Day 3 (page 105)

(5, –2); Two sides of the rectangle are 7 units long and two sides are 3 units long.

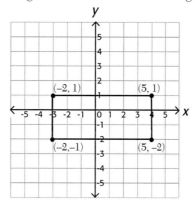

Week 19: Day 4 (page 106)

1. Possible answer:

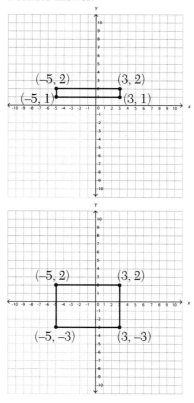

2. Possible answer: The rectangles are similar because they both have two side lengths measuring 8 units each and the opposite side lengths are equal. The rectangles have different side lengths and vertices.

Week 19: Day 5 (page 107)

Student should have plotted and labeled the coordinates on each coordinate plane. The square flag must have all four sides measuring 6 units. The rectangle flag must have two sides measuring 6 units, and the other two sides must be equal in length.

Week 20: Day 1 (page 108)

1. The exponent is 3. The exponent tells you how many times to multiply the base number by itself.

2. $x \bullet x \bullet x$

3. Isabel is incorrect. The equation is asking to find $x \bullet x \bullet x$. So, 9 • 3 is not the same as $x \bullet x \bullet x$. If the base number was 9, the expanded form would be 9 • 9 • 9, which is much greater than 27.

Week 20: Day 2 (page 109)

1. $x = 3$; 3 • 3 • 3 = 27; find a number when multiplied by itself 3 times equals 27

2. $x = 4$; $3^4 = 81$; multiply 3 by itself until it equals 81

Week 20: Day 3 (page 110)

$A = 6x \bullet 6x = 36x^2$; $A = 36(\frac{1}{3})^2 = 36(\frac{1}{9}) = 4$ square units

Week 20: Day 4 (page 111)

1. Possible answers: $3^3 - 3 = 27 - 3 = 24$;
   $5^2 - 1 = 25 - 1 = 24$;
   $2(2^2 + 2^2 + 2^2) = 2(4 + 4 + 4) = 2(12) = 24$

2. Possible answer: I started with familiar exponents and then added, subtracted, multiplied, or divided to arrive at 24.

Week 20: Day 5 (page 112)

1. $2^8 \bullet 5$

2. $2^8 \bullet 5 = 1{,}280$ bacteria

3. $2^{10} \bullet 5 = 5{,}120$ bacteria

4. $3^8 \bullet 5 = 32{,}805$ bacteria

ANSWER KEY *(cont.)*

Week 21: Day 1 (page 113)

1. h; number of hours
2. Laura's reasoning is incorrect. The $15 is a onetime fee, it is not charged every hour. Cory would be overcharging the clients.
3. Cory will use addition because the $15 fee must be added on. He will also use multiplication because the $12 must be multiplied by the number of hours he spends tutoring.

Week 21: Day 2 (page 114)

1. $15 + 12h$; $87; $15 + 12(6) = 87$; write an expression and use h to represent the number of hours
2. $18.50 + 8.50s$; $52.50; $18.50 + 8.50(4) = 52.50$; write an expression and use s to represent the number of students

Week 21: Day 3 (page 115)

Word phrase	Algebraic expression
8 more than the product of 5 and a number	$8 + 5n$
10 less than the quotient of a number and 4	$\frac{n}{4} - 10$
Four times the difference of a number and 6	$4(n - 6)$
Three times the sum of 9 and a number	$3(9 + n)$
a number divided by 2; or the quotient of a number and 2	$\frac{n}{2}$
2 less than the product of 11 and a number	$11n - 2$

Week 21: Day 4 (page 116)

1. Possible expressions: $7.50n + 12n$ or $(7.50 + 12)n$; $19.50n = 19.50(5) = 97.50
2. Possible answer: Both expressions multiply the cost of a movie ticket and a combo by the number of people. The first expression multiplies the cost of a ticket by the number of people and adds this amount to the product of a combo and the number of people. The second expression adds the cost of a ticket and a combo and then multiplies the sum by the number of people.

Week 21: Day 5 (page 117)

1. $75 + 5n + 8n$ or $75 + 13n$
2. $335.00; $75 + 13(20) = 335$
3. $90 + 5n + 8n$ or $90 + 13n$; $350; $75 + 15 + 13n = 90 + 13n$; $90 + 13(20) = 350$
4. $415.00; $90 + 13(20 + 5) = 415$

Week 22: Day 1 (page 118)

1. Yes, there will be a variable in the expression for area. There is a variable in one of the dimensions to which a value has not been assigned.
2. Multiplication
3. The constants are a width of 8 and 4 in the length.

Week 22: Day 2 (page 119)

$8(x + 4) = 8x + 32$ square units; find the area by multiplying the length and the width

Week 22: Day 3 (page 120)

$5(x + 3) = 5$ groups of $x + 3$; $5(x + 3) = 5x + 15$

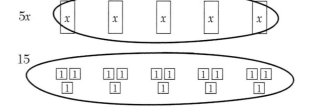

Week 22: Day 4 (page 121)

1. Possible expressions: $3n + 12 = 3(5) + 12 = 27$;
   $3(n + 4) = 3(5 + 4) = 27$;
   $2n + n + 12 = 2(5) + 1(5) + 12 = 27$;
   $n + n + n + 12 = 5 + 5 + 5 + 12 = 27$;
   $n + n + n + 8 + 4 = 5 + 5 + 5 + 8 + 4 = 27$
2. Possible answer: I think $3n + 12$ is easier to solve because it is completely simplified, so it requires fewer steps than solving $n + n + n + 12$.

ANSWER KEY *(cont.)*

Week 22: Day 5 (page 122)

1. Choices A, B, C, and E are accurate. Possible answer: I proved each expression by rewriting it in simplest form, and each correct choice is simplified to $12n$.

2. Choice D is not accurate because the correct expressions should simplify to $12n$. Since $5n$ and 1 are not like terms, they cannot be combined. This expression simplifies to $10n + 2$, not $12n$.

3. Possible answer: I recommend $6n + 4n + 2n$ because it shows how much money Daniel is making from each individual item.

Week 23: Day 1 (page 123)

1. Yes, Clayton has enough cheese to use exactly 100 slices or less.

2. The terms $4s$ and $8l$ use multiplication because the number of slices is multiplied by the number of sandwiches.

3. An inequality states that one value is greater than or less than another value, as well as equal to.

Week 23: Day 2 (page 124)

Choices B, D, and E result in less than or equal to 100 slices of cheese; B. $4(10) + 8(5) \leq 100$; D. $4(20) + 8(2) \leq 100$; E. $4(15) + 8(5) \leq 100$; substitute the values in each answer choice to determine which make the inequality true

Week 23: Day 3 (page 125)

$29 + s = 96$; $s = 67$; Check: $29 + 67 = 96$; $96 = 96$

96	
29	s

Week 23: Day 4 (page 126)

1. $56 > 7n$; Any number less than (but not including) 8 will make the inequality true; Possible answers: $56 > 7 \times 7$; $56 > 49$; or $56 > 7 \times 5\frac{1}{2}$; $56 > 38\frac{1}{2}$

2. Possible answer: There are many more than two solutions that will make the inequality true. Any number less than (but not including) 8 will make the inequality true, including rational numbers (fractions and decimals), for example: $6\frac{3}{4}$, 5.5, and $2\frac{1}{10}$.

Week 23: Day 5 (page 127)

Choices B and C are within the 50 pounds or less weight requirement. Choices A, D, and E are not within the 50 pounds or less weight requirement. Possible answers:

A. $1(10) + 2(10) + 4(10) + 1.5(10) + 5 = 10 + 20 + 40 + 15 + 5 = 90$, which is not less than or equal to 50

B. $1(5) + 2(5) + 4(5) + 1.5(5) + 5 = 5 + 10 + 20 + 7.5 + 5 = 47.5$, which is less than or equal to 50

C. $1(8) + 2(4) + 4(4) + 1.5(4) + 5 = 8 + 8 + 16 + 6 + 5 = 43$, which is less than or equal to 50

D. $1(2) + 2(4) + 4(6) + 1.5(8) + 5 = 2 + 8 + 24 + 12 + 5 = 51$, which is not less than or equal to 50

E. $1(6) + 2(7) + 4(8) + 1.5(0) + 5 = 6 + 14 + 32 + 0 + 5$ is 57, which is not less than or equal to 50

Week 24: Day 1 (page 128)

1. h; number of hours Toula works

2. Multiplication will be used to multiply the number of hours by \$12. Addition will be used to add the \$15 bonus.

3. No, expressions do not include an equal sign. Equations have equal signs (=). If the number of hours Toula worked was given, then her pay can be calculated by writing an equation with an equal sign.

Week 24: Day 2 (page 129)

1. $12h + 15$; write an expression using h to represent the number of hours; use multiplication to represent how much money Toula earns per hour and add this amount to her bonus

2. $16h + 50 - 20$; or $16h + 30$; write an expression using h to represent the number of hours; use multiplication to represent how much money Sumate earns per hour; add the amount he makes in tips; subtract the amount he pays the busboy

ANSWER KEY *(cont.)*

Week 24: Day 3 (page 130)

Possible answer:

The county fair charges $4 for a ride-all-day wristband, plus $0.75 for each line a guest wants to skip with no waiting. Write an expression to represent the amount due for a guest who wants to go on rides.		
Variable	**Definition of variable**	**Expression**
l	number of lines skipped with no waiting	$4 + 0.75l$

Week 24: Day 4 (page 131)

1. Each situation must have the variable defined, multiplication of the variable by 8, and a onetime subtraction of 7. Possible answers: Mia was shopping for T-shirts. She paid $8 for each T-shirt, and had a $7 off coupon. The n represents the number of T-shirts Mia purchased. The expression $8n - 7$ represents the total amount Mia paid for the T-shirts after the coupon discount was subtracted
    Robert is a dog walker. He earns $8 for each dog he walks. From his earnings, he needs to pay his sister back $7 he borrowed from her last week. The n represents the number of dogs Robert walks. The expression $8n - 7$ represents the total amount of money Robert has left from his earnings after he pays back his sister.

2. Possible answer: The problem situations are similar because each situation requires multiplying the variable by 8, and then subtracting 7. They have different contexts and the variable n represents something different.

Week 24: Day 5 (page 132)

1. $s \div 9$ or $\frac{1}{9}s$; Rochelle has 9 times as many superhero comic books as Pierre. To get Pierre's amount divide Rochelle's amount by 9, or multiply by $\frac{1}{9}$.

2. $t \div 7$ or $\frac{1}{7}t$; Pierre has 7 times as many comic books as Rochelle. To get Rochelle's amount divide Pierre's amount by 7, or multiply by $\frac{1}{7}$.

3. 8 superhero comic books; $72 \div 9 = 8$

4. 6 teen humor comic books; $42 \div 7 = 6$

Week 25: Day 1 (page 133)

1. The variable b (or any letter) can be used. The variable represents the number of boxes of granola bars.

2. Multiplication is used because the number of boxes is multiplied by the cost of one box.

3. Aimee can buy at least 3 boxes because 3 boxes will cost $10.50, which is less than $21.00.

4. Aimee cannot buy at least 10 boxes because 10 boxes will cost $35.00, which is more than $21.00.

Week 25: Day 2 (page 134)

1. $\$3.50b = \$21.00$, where b represents the number of boxes of granola bars; $3.5b = 21$; $b = 21 \div 3.5$; $b = 6$; write an equation using b to represent the number of boxes of granola bars and multiply the cost of a box and b to get the total cost; divide both sides of the equation by 3.5 to find the solution

2. $\$15.80c = \$395$, where c represents the number of calculators; $15.8c = 395$; $c = 395 \div 15.8$; $c = 25$; write an equation using c to represent the number of calculators and multiply the cost of a calculator and c to get the total cost; divide both sides of the equation by 15.8 to find the solution

Week 25: Day 3 (page 135)

$\$22.00 + \$18.95 + m = \$50.00$;
$\$40.95 + m = \$50.00$; $m = \$50.00 - \$40.95$;
$m = \$9.05$

$50		
$22	$18.95	money left on gift card (m)

Week 25: Day 4 (page 136)

1. $4d = 72$, where d represents the number of dogs; $d = 18$; 18 dogs, 4 treats each; Possible strategies: equation; bar model; number line; equal groups model; array model

2. Possible answer: I think using an equation is more efficient. I divided 72 by 4 to get 18 because I know the inverse of multiplication is division.

ANSWER KEY *(cont.)*

Week 25: Day 5 (page 137)

1. $12{,}600 = 360h$, where h represents the number of hours
2. $12{,}600 \div 360 = h$; $h = 35$
3. Possible answer: I used division to solve the problem. I divided both numbers by 10 to eliminate one zero in each number. Then, I divided 1,260 by 36, which is 35.

Week 26: Day 1 (page 138)

1. $100 and $200 are included in the solution arrow so, the rental fee can be $100 and $200. $300 is not included in the solution arrow, so the rental fee cannot be $300.
2. The maximum rental fee is $250. Since there is a solid point above $250, that means $250 is included in the solution.
3. The numbers to the left of zero are negative numbers. It would not make sense for this situation because the community center would not be charging a negative amount of money.

Week 26: Day 2 (page 139)

1. $r \le \$250$; the solution is less than or equal to 250; write an inequality that represents the solution arrow on the number line; include 250 in the solution since there is a solid point in the solution arrow
2. $f \ge \$5$; the solution is greater than or equal to 5; write an inequality that represents the solution arrow on the number line; include 5 in the solution since there is a solid point in the solution arrow

Week 26: Day 3 (page 140)

$m > 15$

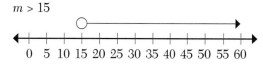

Week 26: Day 4 (page 141)

1. $s \le 20$

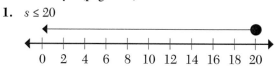

$s < 20$

2. Possible answer: Both inequalities have the variable s to represent the go-kart speed and 20 kilometers per hour is included in each inequality and number line. The first inequality uses the symbol $\le$ and includes 20 in the solution and the second inequality uses the $<$ symbol and does not include 20 in the solution.

Week 26: Day 5 (page 142)

1. $h < 36$; Possible answer:

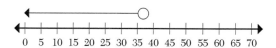

2. $h \ge 44$; Possible answer:

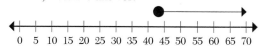

3. Any height from 36–43 inches will not be permitted to enter Kiddie Town or ride Turbo Roller Coaster. Possible answer: A guest who is 40 inches tall is too tall to enter Kiddie Town and too short to ride Turbo Roller Coaster.

Week 27: Day 1 (page 143)

1. The points are not connected because Nick cannot feed a fractional amount of sheep. This is an example of discrete data.
2. The independent variable s is the number of sheep. The independent variable is graphed on the x-axis.
3. The dependent variable h is the number of pounds of hay. The dependent variable is graphed on the y-axis.
4. As the number of sheep increases by 1, the number of pounds of hay increases by 4 pounds.

ANSWER KEY *(cont.)*

Week 27: Day 2 (page 144)

$h = 4s$; write an equation to represent the relationship in the graph; use s to represent the independent variable for the number of sheep; use h to represent the dependent variable for the number of pounds of hay; multiply the independent variable by the rate of change

Week 27: Day 3 (page 145)

$c = 2n$

Games (n)	Cost (c) (in dollars)
1	2
2	4
3	6
4	8
5	10
6	12
7	14
8	16

Kendra's Game Downloads

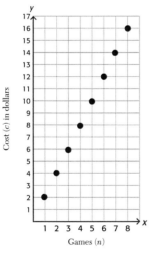

Week 27: Day 4 (page 146)

1. $b = 6r$; Possible answer: $(5, 30)$; $30 = 6(5)$; $30 = 30$

Cups of raisins (r)	Slices of bread (b)
1	6
2	12
3	18
4	24
5	30
6	36
7	42
8	48
9	54
10	60

2. Possible answer: An advantage of using an equation is it can be used to find the quantity given another quantity.

Week 27: Day 5 (page 147)

1.

Hours (n)	Cost (c) in dollars
1	17
2	34
3	51
4	68
5	85

Cost to Rent a Paddleboat

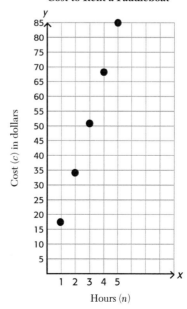

2. $c = 17n$; As the number of hours increases by 1, the cost increases by \$17.

ANSWER KEY *(cont.)*

Week 28: Day 1 (page 148)

1. Lindsey's reasoning is not correct. Multiplying 60 by 26 would give the area of a rectangle with these dimensions, but this is a trapezoid. Simply doing base times height will not give an accurate result of a trapezoid's area.

2. The rectangle is 30 × 26. Each triangle is 15 × 26 × 30.

3. We can add the three areas together to get the total area of the trapezoid.

Week 28: Day 2 (page 149)

1,170 square inches; area of rectangle: 30 × 26 = 780; area of each right triangle: 15 × 26 = 195; area of trapezoid: 780 + 195 + 195 = 1,170; find the area of the rectangle and the area of each triangle, and then add the areas together

Week 28: Day 3 (page 150)

Area of prototype: A = 1 in.²; A = $\frac{1}{2}$(2)(1) = 1; Area of actual magnet: A = 16 in.²; A = $\frac{1}{2}$(8)(4) = 16; The area of the actual magnet is 16 times larger than the prototype.

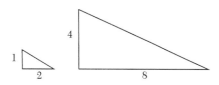

Week 28: Day 4 (page 151)

1. The area is 504 square inches. Possible strategies: make 3 vertical lines to partition the letter "E" into 4 rectangles, find the area of each rectangle, and then add the areas together (324 + 63 + 54 + 63 = 504); draw a vertical line to enclose the letter "E" into one large rectangle, find the area of the entire large rectangle, find the area of each small rectangle that is not part of the letter "E," add the areas that are not part of the letter "E," and then subtract the areas that are not part of the letter "E" from the larger rectangle (648 – 72 – 72 = 504).

2. Possible answer: I think finding the area of the entire large rectangle and then subtracting the areas not part of the letter "E" is more efficient. It took me fewer steps than to partition the letter "E" into rectangles, finding the area of each rectangle, and then adding the areas together.

Week 28: Day 5 (page 152)

1. Student should have drawn a right triangle and labeled the base and height of the triangle with 4 inches. The area of one 4 in. by 4 in. triangular fabric piece is 8 square inches; A = $\frac{1}{2}$(4)(4) = 8 in.²

2. Student should have drawn a large rectangle and converted the 5 ft. by 7 ft. rectangle to 60 inches by 84 inches in order to compare like units. The area of the 60 × 84 quilt is 5,040 square inches; A = 60 × 84 = 5,040 in.²

3. Charity will need 630 fabric pieces; 5,040 ÷ 8 = 630

ANSWER KEY (cont.)

Week 29: Day 1 (page 153)

1. There are 8 halves in 4. There are 6 halves in 3.
2. There are 4 layers of sugar cubes. There are 2 halves, or half inches, in 1 inch. There are 4 halves, or half inches, in 2 inches.
3. Natalie would be correct if the sugar cubes were 1 inch on each side, or 1 inch × 1 inch × 1 inch. But, these sugar cubes are $\frac{1}{2}$ inch on each side, or $\frac{1}{2}$ inch × $\frac{1}{2}$ inch × $\frac{1}{2}$ inch. So, multiplying 4 inches × 3 inches × 2 inches will not give her an accurate number of sugar cubes.

Week 29: Day 2 (page 154)

192 sugar cubes; volume of box: $4 \times 3 \times 2 = 24$; volume of sugar cube: $\frac{1}{2} \times \frac{1}{2} \times \frac{1}{2} = \frac{1}{8}$; $24 \div \frac{1}{8} = 192$; find the volume of the box, find the volume of a sugar cube, and divide the volume of the box by the volume of a sugar cube

Week 29: Day 3 (page 155)

There are 7 layers with 15 cubes in each layer; 105 cubes with dimensions $\frac{1}{4}$ inch × $\frac{1}{4}$ inch × $\frac{1}{4}$ inch are in the prism; student should have labeled the length of the prism $\frac{5}{4}$ in., the width of the prism $\frac{3}{4}$ in., and the height of the prism $\frac{7}{4}$ in.

Week 29: Day 4 (page 156)

1. Possible answer: Student 1 is correct because there are four $\frac{1}{4}$ s in 1 inch ($4 \times 4 \times 4 = 64$). Student 2 is correct because the small cube has a volume of $\frac{1}{4} \times \frac{1}{4} \times \frac{1}{4} = \frac{1}{64}$ cubic inch. So, one small cube must be $\frac{1}{64}$ of the large cube. Or, since 64 of the $\frac{1}{4}$-inch cubes make up the large cube, one of them would be $\frac{1}{64}$ of the large cube.
2. Possible answer: The two answers are similar because each student recognized that there are four $\frac{1}{4}$ s in 1 inch. Student 1 filled in the larger prism with 64 of the $\frac{1}{4}$-inch cubes and student 2 is focusing on just one of the $\frac{1}{4}$-inch cubes.

Week 29: Day 5 (page 157)

1. Volume of mini pie box: $V = \frac{1}{4} \times \frac{1}{4} \times \frac{1}{4} = \frac{1}{64}$ cubic ft.; student should have drawn a sketch of the box and labeled the dimensions
2. Volume of large shipping carton: $V = 2\frac{1}{4} \times 1\frac{3}{4} \times 2 = 7\frac{7}{8}$ cubic ft.; student should have drawn a sketch of the carton and labeled the dimensions
3. 504 pie boxes; Possible answers: $2\frac{1}{4}$ is equal to $\frac{9}{4}$; $1\frac{3}{4}$ is equal to $\frac{7}{4}$; 2 is equal to $\frac{8}{4}$; $9 \times 7 \times 8$ is 504; 504 small $\frac{1}{4}$ in. 3 boxes will fit into a shipping carton; or student may have divided the volume of the carton by the volume of a box; $7\frac{7}{8} \div \frac{1}{64} = 504$

Week 30: Day 1 (page 158)

1. The area is found by multiplying the two dimensions of the base (length and width), and area is the amount of space covered in square units, or units^2. The height is only one dimension, so it is not given in square units.
2. Cubic units, in this case cubic meters or m^3, will be used for volume. Volume is a three-dimensional measurement of how many cubic units make up a figure.
3. The 12 in the problem is the area of the base, not just one dimension. The volume of a rectangular prism can be calculated with the area of the base and the height.

Week 30: Day 2 (page 159)

$\frac{48}{3}$ m^3 or 16 m^3; $V = 12 \times 1\frac{1}{3} = 16$; find the volume of the rectangular prism by multiplying the base and the height

Week 30: Day 3 (page 160)

$81 = 4.5 \times w \times 6$; $81 = 27 \times w$; $w = 3$ ft.; student should have labeled the rectangular prism with a length of 4.5 ft., the width with w, and the height with 6 ft.

Week 30: Day 4 (page 161)

1. The volume of the casserole is 255 in.^{3}; Possible strategies: find the volume of the full pan ($12\frac{3}{4} \times 8 \times 3\frac{1}{2} = 357$ in.^{3}), then the volume of the empty part of the casserole pan ($12\frac{3}{4} \times 8 \times 1 = 102$ in.^{3}), and finally subtracting the empty pan volume from the full pan volume for a result of 255 in.^{3}; or use $2\frac{1}{2}$ as the height instead of $3\frac{1}{2}$, since the top 1-inch of the pan must be left empty ($\frac{3}{4} \times 8 \times 2\frac{1}{2} = 255$ in.^{3})
2. Possible answer: I think it is more efficient to subtract 1 inch from the height of $3\frac{1}{2}$ and then find the volume of the casserole. I only need to find the volume once using the new dimensions of $12\frac{3}{4} \times 8 \times 2\frac{1}{2}$.

Week 30: Day 5 (page 162)

1. $10{,}842\frac{3}{4}$ in.^{3}; $30\frac{1}{2} \times 18 \times 19\frac{3}{4} = 10{,}842\frac{3}{4}$
2. $2{,}196$ in.^{3}; $V = 30\frac{1}{2} \times 18 \times 4 = 2{,}196$
3. $8{,}646\frac{3}{4}$ in.^{3}; Possible answer: $30\frac{1}{2} \times 18 \times 15\frac{3}{4} = 8{,}646\frac{3}{4}$ in.^{3} I used $15\frac{3}{4}$ instead of $19\frac{3}{4}$ because 4 of those inches are covered in bedding material. I subtracted the 4 inches of bedding material to get a new height.

ANSWER KEY *(cont.)*

Week 31: Day 1 (page 163)

1. 6 faces
2. Each face is a square because all of the sides are equal.
3. A cube because all six of the faces are squares.
4. Curtis is incorrect. He found the volume. He needs to find the surface area.

Week 31: Day 2 (page 164)

The surface area is 294 cm; 49 + 49 + 49 + 49 + 49 + 49 = 294 cm^2 or 6 × 49 = 294 cm^2; find the area of each face and then add the areas together to find the surface area

Week 31: Day 3 (page 165)

Area of square base = 2 × 2 = 4 cm^2
Area of four triangular faces = 4 × ($\frac{1}{2}$ × 2 × 2) = 8 cm.^{2}
Area of square pyramid = 4 + 8 = 12 cm^2

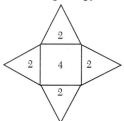

Week 31: Day 4 (page 166)

1. The surface area of each net is 2,376 in.^{2}; Possible nets:

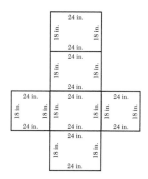

2. Possible answer: The shapes of the two nets are similar because each net includes two 18 in. × 18 in. squares and four 18 in. by 24 in. rectangles, and the surface area of each net is the same (2,376 in.^{2}). The placement of the faces is different in the two nets.

Week 31: Day 5 (page 167)

1. Possible net:

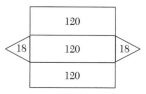

2. 396 in.^{2}; Possible answer: There are two 6 × 6 triangles, each with an area of 18 in.^{2}. There are three 20 × 6 rectangles, each with an area of 120 in.^{2} When added together, 18 + 18 + 120 + 120 + 120 = 396 in.^{2}

ANSWER KEY *(cont.)*

Week 32: Day 1 (page 168)

1. The only responses to Lucy's question would be "yes" or "no."
2. There are many different possible responses to Walter's question. Any number of minutes can be an answer.
3. Possible answer: A statistical question identifies a specific population and requires a variety of responses.

Week 32: Day 2 (page 169)

Walter submits the statistical question. He identified the specific population of students. His question asks for a specific number of minutes students spend doing homework each night. A variety of different responses can be included in the question.

Week 32: Day 3 (page 170)

1. Possible answers:

Statistical question	Non-statistical question
How many hours per day do sixth graders at my school watch television?	What is your favorite television show?
How many minutes per week do the members of the school basketball team practice outside of required practices?	Are you on the basketball team?

2. Possible answer: A statistical question includes a specific population and there are many different responses. A non-statistical question only asks "you" a question, and allows only one answer or a yes/no answer.

Week 32: Day 4 (page 171)

1. Questions should include a topic, population, and variability. Possible answers: How many minutes per week do book club members want to spend reading our book?; How many books per month do book club members read that are not part of the book club?; How many meetings per month do club members prefer to attend?
2. Possible answer: The statistical questions I wrote are similar because they have a specific topic, a specific population, and allow for many different responses.

Week 32: Day 5 (page 172)

Possible answers:

1. What percentage of students at each grade level at Maple Middle School has access to a computer at home?
2. How many students at Maple Middle School have Internet access outside of school?
3. What is the typical number of apps students at Maple Middle School have on their devices?
4. What proportion of students at Maple Middle School use a computer to complete school work?
5. How many minutes per week do students at Maple Middle School spend playing computer games?

Week 33: Day 1 (page 173)

1. Each X represents one student.
2. There is one X above 0 to show that this student bought 0 lunches that week.
3. The line plot has a maximum number of 5 because there are 5 days in the school week, so students can buy their lunch a maximum of 5 times in that week.
4. Possible questions: What is the mean of the data? What is the median of the data?

Week 33: Day 2 (page 174)

Students buy lunch from 0 to 5 times per week. The line plot skews toward the right, and peaks at 5 times per week. The median is 4, so 50% of the students buy lunch 4 times per week or less and 50% of the students buy lunch 4 times per week or more. The mean is 3.53, meaning if the data was balanced to show that the students bought their lunch the same number of times per week, they would each buy it 3.6 times.

ANSWER KEY *(cont.)*

Week 33: Day 3 (page 175)

Scores in order from least to greatest: 0, 1, 2, 2, 2, 3, 3, 3, 4; The minimum score is 0. The maximum score is 4. The median is 2. For the lower 50% of the scores, the median is 1.5 (or $1\frac{1}{2}$). For the upper 50% of the scores, the median is 3.

Written Response Scores from Emily's Language Arts Class

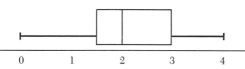

Week 33: Day 4 (page 176)

1. Jane used the mean to describe the data. Jane balanced the data to show the number of minutes band members would practice if they each practiced the same number of minutes. This number is 17.5 minutes each. Elizabeth used the median to describe the data. Elizabeth found the middle point of the data, showing that 50% of the band members practice 15 minutes or less, and that 50% of the band members practice 15 minutes or more.

2. Possible answers: The median shows the number of minutes that band members typically practice, with 50% practicing 15 minutes or less and 50% practicing 15 minutes or more. Or, the mean shows the number of minutes each band member would practice if they each practiced the same number of minutes.

Week 33: Day 5 (page 177)

1. **North Middle School Hawks Baskekball Players**

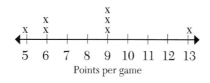

Points per game

2.

South Middle School Eagles Baskekball Players

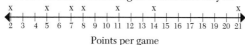

Points per game

3. Possible answer: The players from North Middle School score from 5 to 13 points. The players from South Middle School score from 2 to 21 points. The NMS data is centered at 9 and is more closely arranged. The SMS data is centered at 8, but is very spread out.

Week 34: Day 1 (page 178)

1. 14 members are included in the sample because I added up the heights of each bar in the histogram: 4 + 2 + 1 + 1 + 4 + 2 = 14.

2. Zero (0) is included on the histogram because 4 members in the sample did not spend any time warming up.

3. Median; find the data point in the middle

4. Mean; find the average of the data points by adding them together and dividing by the number of data points

Week 34: Day 2 (page 179)

Variance or range: 5; the times vary 5 minutes between the least and greatest number of minutes spent warming up; midpoint or median: 3 minutes; balancing point or mean: $2\frac{7}{15}$ (or approximately 2.467 minutes; 2 minutes, 28 seconds)

Week 34: Day 3 (page 180)

Center: The median is 4 DVDs. The mean is $3\frac{11}{20}$ (or 3.55) DVDs. Variance: The range, or difference between the greatest number of DVDs and least number of DVDs checked out, is 4.

Library DVD Check Out

DVD's checked out

ANSWER KEY *(cont.)*

Week 34: Day 4 (page 181)

1. Line plots should include 18 Xs, a variance of 8, and a median of 5; Possible line plots:

   The mean of the data is $5\frac{2}{18}$ or $5\frac{1}{9}$ (or about 5.11) letters.

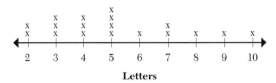

Length of First Names

Letters

   The mean of the data is $5\frac{15}{18}$ or $5\frac{5}{6}$ (or approximately 5.83) letters.

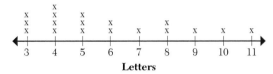

Length of First Names

Letters

2. Possible answer: The two line plots are similar because there are 18 Xs to represent the 18 students. The median is 5. The lengths of the first names are different and the number of Xs for each length varies.

Week 34: Day 5 (page 182)

Possible answers: Our reviews on Yum Yum vary by 5 stars. Our reviews on Suppertime Stars vary by 2 stars. The ratings on Suppertime Stars are more consistent because the data is closer together and varies less. Yum Yum's median (midpoint) is 4. Suppertime Stars' median (midpoint) is 3. Our median is higher on Yum Yum because of so many 4- and 5-star ratings. Yum Yum's mean (balancing point) is $2\frac{20}{25}$, or 2.8 stars. Suppertime Stars' mean (balancing point) is $3\frac{1}{25}$, or 3.04, stars. Our mean is higher on Suppertime Stars because we have many 3- and 4-star ratings. We have no 5s, but no 0s either.

Week 35: Day 1 (page 183)

1. 50%
2. 50%
3. No, there is no way to tell exactly how many dogs Trina has. The box plot is giving a summary of the weights and the general shape of the data.
4. Possible questions: What is the median of the data? What is the range of the weights?

Week 35: Day 2 (page 184)

Five number summary: the minimum weight is 70 pounds; Quartile 1 is 76 pounds; Quartile 2 (or median) is 82 pounds; Quartile 3 is 89 pounds; The maximum weight is 95 pounds; Possible answer: 25% of the dogs are from 70–76 pounds; 50% of the dogs are from 70–82 pounds; 50% of the dogs are from 82–95 pounds; 25% of the dogs are from 89–95 pounds; The lightest dog is 70 pounds; The heaviest dog is 95 pounds.

Week 35: Day 3 (page 185)

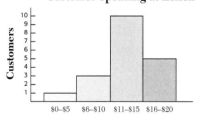

Customer Spending at Lunch

ANSWER KEY *(cont.)*

Week 35: Day 4 (page 186)

1. Appropriate graphs are a line plot and a box plot. A histogram is not appropriate to this data because histograms show continuous data. Loads of laundry are not continuous data as no one is doing a fractional load of laundry. Possible graphs:

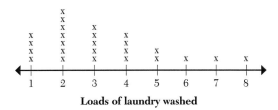

Loads Washed at Sudsy Laundromat

Loads of laundry washed

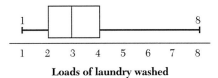

Loads Washed at Sudsy Laundromat

Loads of laundry washed

2. Possible answer: I decided to use a line plot and a box plot. The line plot shows that the data peaks at 2 loads. The box plot shows the median, minimum, maximum, and where the data is grouped. The median is 3 loads of laundry. Fifty percent of the customers did between 2 and 4 loads of laundry, 25 did between 1 and 2 loads, and 25% did between 4 and 8 loads.

Week 35: Day 5 (page 187)

1.

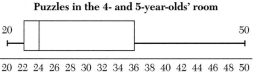

Puzzles in the 2- and 3-year-olds' room

Pieces in the puzzles

2.

Puzzles in the 4- and 5-year-olds' room

Pieces in the puzzles

Week 36: Day 1 (page 188)

1. Find the missing weight (ounces) of Swiss cheese that will make the weights in the list of items result in a mean of 24 ounces.

2. The weights of the other five items and the required mean of 24 ounces are given.

3. This situation is different because in previous problems, the mean was calculated. In this situation, the mean is given. Instead of finding the mean, the problem is asking to find a specific data point that will result in the given mean.

ANSWER KEY *(cont.)*

Week 36: Day 2 (page 189)

18 ounces of Swiss cheese; the mean of 24 ounces multiplied by 6 total items is 144 ounces; when the five known items are added together, the sum is 126 ounces; 144 – 126 = 18

Week 36: Day 3 (page 190)

Weight of hot-food assortment (in ounces)	Distance of each weight from the mean (deviation)	Positive distance from the mean (absolute deviation)
34	34 – 36 = –2	2
38	38 – 36 = 2	2
42	42 – 36 = 6	6
48	48 – 36 = 12	12
16	16 – 36 = –20	20
Sum of the weights: 178		Sum of the absolute deviations: 42
Mean of the weights: 178 ÷ 5 = 35.6		Mean absolute deviation: 42 ÷ 5 = 8.4

Week 36: Day 4 (page 191)

1. In general, each amount varies by 3 pictures above or below the mean of 12 pictures; Range: Since the data ranges from 7–18, the number of pictures varies by 11 between the least and greatest value; Mean absolute deviation: Since the MAD is 3, that means the photographers were 3 pictures above or below the mean of 12 pictures.

Number of pictures taken	Distance from the mean (deviation)	Positive distance from the mean (absolute deviation)
16	16 – 12 = 4	4
10	10 – 12= –2	2
8	8 – 12= –4	4
14	14 – 12= 2	2
18	18 – 12= 6	6
12	12 – 12 = 0	0
11	11 – 12= –1	1
7	7 – 12 = –5	5
Sum of the pictures: 96		Sum of the absolute deviations: 24
Mean of the pictures: 96 ÷ 8 = 12		Mean absolute deviation: 24 ÷ 8 = 3

2. Possible answer: The range tells me that the data varies by 11 pictures. The MAD of 3 tells me that on average, the photographers were 3 pictures above or below the mean of 12 pictures. The MAD gives more specific information, so I think it is more useful.

ANSWER KEY *(cont.)*

Week 36: Day 5 (page 192)

Weight of plain yogurt (in ounces)	Distance of each weight from the mean (deviation)	Positive distance from the mean (absolute deviation)
7	7 – 8 = –1	1
6	6 – 8 = –2	2
8	8 – 8 = 0	0
10	10 – 8 = 2	2
10	10 – 8 = 2	2
12	12 – 8 = 4	4
6	6 – 8 = –2	2
9	9 – 8 = 1	1
6	6 – 8 = –2	2
6	6 – 8 = –2	2
Sum of the weights: 80		Sum of the absolute deviations: 18
Mean of the weights: 80 ÷ 10 = 8		Mean absolute deviation: 18 ÷ 10 = 1.8

Weight of yogurt with toppings (in ounces)	Distance of each weight from the mean (deviation)	Positive distance from the mean (absolute deviation)
14	14 – 14 = 0	0
15	15 – 14 = 1	1
16	16 – 14 = 2	2
10	10 – 14 = –4	4
20	20 – 14 = 6	6
11	11 – 14 = –3	3
11	11 – 14 = –3	3
18	18 – 14 = 4	4
12	12 – 14 = –2	2
13	13 – 14 = –1	1
Sum of the weights: 140		Sum of the absolute deviations: 26
Mean of the weights: 140 ÷ 10 = 14		Mean absolute deviation: 26 ÷ 10 = 2.6

PRACTICE PAGE RUBRIC

Directions: Evaluate student work in each category by choosing one number in each row. Students have opportunities to score up to four points in each row and up to 16 points total.

	Advanced	**Proficient**	**Developing**	**Beginning**
Problem-solving strategies	Uses multiple efficient strategies Uses a detailed and appropriate visual model	Uses appropriate strategies Uses an appropriate visual model	Demonstrates some form of strategic approach Uses a visual model but is incomplete	No strategic approach is evident No visual model is attempted
Points	4	3	2	1
Mathematical knowledge	Provides correct solutions and multiple solutions when relevant Connects and applies the concept in complex ways	Provides correct solutions Demonstrates proficiency of concept	Shows some correct solutions Demonstrates some proficiency of concept	No solutions are correct Does not demonstrate proficiency of concept
Points	4	3	2	1
Explanation	Explains and justifies thinking thoroughly and clearly	Explains and justifies thinking	Explains thinking but difficult to follow	Offers no explanation of thinking
Points	4	3	2	1
Organization	Well-planned, well-organized, and complete	Shows a plan and is complete	Shows some planning and is mostly complete	Shows no planning and is mostly incomplete
Points	4	3	2	1

PRACTICE PAGE ITEM ANALYSIS

Directions: Record students' rubric scores (page 219) for the Day 5 practice page in the appropriate columns. Add the totals and record the sums in the Total Scores column. You can view: (1) which students are not understanding the mathematical concepts and problem-solving steps, and (2) how students progress after multiple encounters with the problem-solving process.

Student Name	Week 1	Week 2	Week 3	Week 4	Week 5	Week 6	Week 7	Week 8	Week 9	Total Scores
Average Class Score										

PRACTICE PAGE ITEM ANALYSIS *(cont.)*

Directions: Record students' rubric scores (page 219) for the Day 5 practice page in the appropriate columns. Add the totals and record the sums in the Total Scores column. You can view: (1) which students are not understanding the mathematical concepts and problem-solving steps, and (2) how students progress after multiple encounters with the problem-solving process.

Student Name	Week 10	Week 11	Week 12	Week 13	Week 14	Week 15	Week 16	Week 17	Week 18	Total Scores
Average Class Score										

PRACTICE PAGE ITEM ANALYSIS *(cont.)*

Directions: Record students' rubric scores (page 219) for the Day 5 practice page in the appropriate columns. Add the totals and record the sums in the Total Scores column. You can view: (1) which students are not understanding the mathematical concepts and problem-solving steps, and (2) how students progress after multiple encounters with the problem-solving process.

Student Name	Week 19	Week 20	Week 21	Week 22	Week 23	Week 24	Week 25	Week 26	Week 27	Total Scores
Average Class Score										

PRACTICE PAGE ITEM ANALYSIS *(cont.)*

Directions: Record students' rubric scores (page 219) for the Day 5 practice page in the appropriate columns. Add the totals and record the sums in the Total Scores column. You can view: (1) which students are not understanding the mathematical concepts and problem-solving steps, and (2) how students progress after multiple encounters with the problem-solving process.

Student Name	Week 28	Week 29	Week 30	Week 31	Week 32	Week 33	Week 34	Week 35	Week 36	Total Scores
Average Class Score										

STUDENT ITEM ANALYSIS

Directions: Record individual student's rubric scores (page 219) for each practice page in the appropriate columns. Add the totals and record the sums in the Total Scores column. You can view: (1) which concepts and problem-solving steps the student is not understanding and (2) how the student is progressing after multiple encounters with the problem-solving process.

Student Name:						
	Day 1	Day 2	Day 3	Day 4	Day 5	Total Scores
Week 1						
Week 2						
Week 3						
Week 4						
Week 5						
Week 6						
Week 7						
Week 8						
Week 9						
Week 10						
Week 11						
Week 12						
Week 13						
Week 14						
Week 15						
Week 16						
Week 17						
Week 18						
Week 19						
Week 20						
Week 21						
Week 22						
Week 23						
Week 24						
Week 25						
Week 26						
Week 27						
Week 28						
Week 29						
Week 30						
Week 31						
Week 32						
Week 33						
Week 34						
Week 35						
Week 36						

PROBLEM-SOLVING FRAMEWORK

Use the following problem-solving steps to help you:

1. understand the problem

2. make a plan

3. solve the problem

4. check your answer and explain your thinking

What Do You Know?

- read/reread the problem

- restate the problem in your own words

- visualize the problem

- find the important information in the problem

- understand what the question is asking

What Is Your Plan?

- draw a picture or model

- decide which strategy to use

- choose an operation $(+, -, \times, \div)$

- determine if there is one step or multiple steps

Solve the Problem!

- carry out your plan

- check your steps as you are solving the problem

- decide if your strategy is working or choose a new strategy

- find the solution to the problem

Look Back and Explain!

- check that your solution makes sense and is reasonable

- determine if there are other possible solutions

- use words to explain your solution

PROBLEM-SOLVING STRATEGIES

Draw a picture or diagram.	Make a table or list.	Use a number sentence or formula.
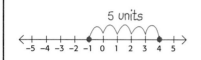 5 units		$\frac{1}{5} + \frac{2}{5} = \frac{3}{5}$ $A = l \times w$

Make a model.	Look for a pattern.	Act it out.
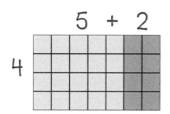 5 + 2 4	 3, 6, 12, 24, 48, __96__	

Solve a simpler problem.	Work backward.	Use logical reasoning.
6×8 $6 \times 4 \times 2$ 24×2 48	 $\boxed{} \times 3 \times 5 = 30$	

Guess and check.	Create a graph.	Use concrete objects.
$2 \times \boxed{} + 5 = 13$ $2 \times 4 + 5 = 13$ $13 = 13$ Yes!	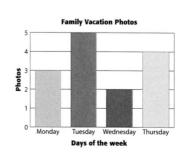	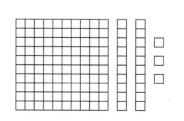 base-ten blocks

DIGITAL RESOURCES

Teacher Resources

Resource	Filename
Practice Page Rubric	rubric.pdf
Practice Page Item Analysis	itemanalysis.pdf itemanalysis.docx itemanalysis.xlsx
Student Item Analysis	studentitem.pdf studentitem.docx studentitem.xlsx

Student Resources

Resource	Filename
Problem-Solving Framework	framework.pdf
Problem-Solving Strategies	strategies.pdf

NOTES

NOTES

NOTES

NOTES

NOTES